MW01256270

# The Diary
# Of An
# *Intrepid*
# Home Inspector

Stories that will entertain and inform you

**If you are a home buyer or owner**

- Buy the right house the first time or the next time
- Choose the right professionals to help you buy a house
- Better understand the house you now own

**If you are or want to become a home inspector**

- Benefit from the experiences of a veteran home inspector
- Learn some "tricks of the trade"

**If you are a real estate agent**

- Understand the home inspector  perspective
- Use home inspectors for your benefit

By: Rudy Platzer

With:  Ruth E Schneider

Copyright © 2012, PS Enterprises

All rights reserved.  No part of this book may be reproduced in any form without the express written consent of the author or his successors. Address requests to RudyPlatzer@aol.com

PS Press
First Printing 2012

Additional copies may be purchased directly from the publisher at the following link:
http://www.lulu.com/shop/rudy-platzer/the-diary-of-an-intrepid-home-inspector/paperback/product-20259053.html

ISBN: 9780557625192

First Edition
Printed in the United States of America

# Acknowledgements

This book is dedicated to:

- The memory of my parents, who inspired me to become an American Patriot, and taught me that I could be anything I wanted to be through hard work and perseverance.

- The memory of my mentors, John Cox and M. B. "Speed" Williams, who taught me that I really didn't know everything and challenged me to keep learning and practicing.

- My friend Brian Normile, who encouraged me to become an inspector and who eagerly read and proofed manuscripts.

- Many other good friends and fellow inspectors who offered suggestions and encouraged me to follow-through on this book. Their enthusiasm and willingness to get involved in the details of this project inspired me to continue writing and to finally publish this book.

- Ruth, the love of my life, for her help in writing this book and for helping me to establish, build and operate my successful home inspection business over the years.

# Contents

# INTRODUCTION

## About This Book

My 25 years as a home inspector was an exciting time in my life. As I told people stories of the situations I encountered, they often said, "You should write a book!" So, here it is.

I've inspected over 6,000 homes. I've evaluated everything from mobile homes, condominiums, and starter homes, to palatial estates; from new construction to national historic treasures. I've worked with attorneys in lawsuits against builders, remodelers, contractors, real estate agents, home inspectors and sellers. I've worked for buyers, sellers, attorneys, real estate agents, corporations and charitable foundations. Through it all I was driven by a life-long curiosity about how things work and a desire to help people. Home inspection was truly a career that called upon everything I had ever learned and often caused me to scratch my head and learn even more. And, I had so much satisfaction along the way — meeting all kinds of people, offering advice, and learning from every experience.

I've written this book as a series of very short vignettes. You can read the ones that most interest you, in any order. My intent is to educate and to entertain as I recall a few of the many memorable experiences I had during a very satisfying career.

This book is written especially for home buyers and for anyone who is, has been or wants to become a home inspector. It will also be beneficial to home owners, home sellers, real estate brokers and agents. Others will hopefully just find the real life stories interesting and entertaining.


*Rudy Platzer BS, MA,*
Certified ASHI® Inspector #1956 (retired)

# About The Author

Rudy Platzer is a proud American! He was taught by his parents and teachers that he could be anything he aspired to be in this wonderful land of opportunity. He worked hard pursuing excellence, and success followed.

Rudy grew up in a working class neighborhood in Dayton Ohio, the son of immigrant parents with eighth grade educations. Although it was a rough part of town, he managed to break out — singing solo soprano in the Dayton Boys' Choir and writing poems published in the National Anthology of Poetry. He also played drum solos at a number of public events.

None of the men in his family had ever finished high school, but his mother convinced him to take college preparatory courses, "just in case." At age 14, to help with family expenses, he took an after-school job building cabinets and counter tops in a custom woodworking shop. He built a kneehole desk out of scrap lumber, which he still uses in his office. While in high school, he organized and led a very popular dance band. He joined the American Federation of Musicians at age 18 and continued his part-time music career for 50 years, a hobby of love. After graduating with honors from high school, in the midst of a severe economic recession, the only job he could find was in a local foundry as an unskilled laborer. He was hospitalized with a life threatening illness, partly because of the horrible factory environment, and when he recovered he decided it was time to go to college. He had been able to save some money and entered the University of Dayton two years out of high school. He paid his tuition and living expenses by working part-time as a furniture repairman and refinisher at local furniture stores. He also drove a taxi cab (perhaps "The Diary of an Intrepid Cab Driver" will be his next book!) On weekends he played with the popular local big bands of the day. He had planned on receiving a regular Army Officer's commission after completing his ROTC commitment, but instead suffered multiple injuries in a work related accident and became physically disqualified for military service. Upon graduation with a degree in business organization and philosophy, he took a position with the Federal government where he served as a civilian in Air Force Intelligence for most of his 30 year career — an exciting and rewarding experience which he loved. For his contributions, he was presented the Air Force Exceptional Civilian Service Award, the highest honor granted an Air Force civilian — a recognition rarely awarded. He retired as a Technical Director in the Foreign Technology Division at Wright-Patterson Air Force Base in Ohio.

Upon retiring from the Air Force, he established a home inspection company which he operated for 25 years. He inspected over 6,000 residential and commercial structures for well-satisfied clients.

Over the years his avocation has been building single and multiple family housing and custom homes. He also restored two historic buildings and remodeled several others.

He served as President of the Ohio Chapter of the American Society of Home Inspectors (ASHI) as well as serving on the ASHI International Board of Directors. His practice is now limited to advising attorneys on cases involving construction defects and providing expert witness testimony in related court trials.

Rudy holds both Bachelor and Master degrees in business and is a graduate of the Industrial College of the Armed Forces. He holds a certificate from the Professional Inspectors Training Institute and is also a licensed US Coast Guard Captain. He resides in Marblehead, Ohio with his partner and best friend of 29 years, Ruth Schneider, and their two loveable cats, "Gus " and "Elsa."

# A Brief History of the Home Inspection Profession

When I entered the profession, in the 1980s, very few people thought about having a home inspected. Some friends, Brian and Mary Normile, were traveling by car in another state, and heard a spot radio ad for a home inspection service. They called me when they returned home to tell me about it. This would be a perfect retirement job for me, they thought. I thought so, too. I had built houses and apartment buildings and had managed government construction projects. "I can do this easily", I thought. So I began to do some research.

I heard about the American Society of Home Inspectors (ASHI®) — which was organized by a small group of home inspectors on the east coast of the U.S. in 1976. These pioneers wanted to better serve consumers by establishing standards of performance and ethical criteria for the infant industry, and by educating each other through a continuing series of educational meetings. These dedicated professionals concentrated on the technical side of the business — how to provide the best possible professional defect disclosure to home buyers.

I had the pleasure and honor of studying under two of these pioneers, John Cox and M.B. "Speed" Williams, who founded the Professional Home Inspectors Training Institute. Through my continued professional relationship with these men I was able to tap into the ultra-professionalism of the early ASHI group. They were my heroes then and now! From them I learned that there was so much more to learn! Realizing the challenges which lay ahead, I studied the home inspection business intensely for a year before I attempted my first inspection.

Today, as then, ASHI® is the standard bearer for the home inspection industry. Over time it has refined its Standards of Practice and Code of Ethics — which are widely accepted as industry hallmarks. ASHI® members agree to conduct their business in accordance with these guidelines.

ASHI® membership is voluntary. To be accepted as a Certified Member strict experience, testing and performance requirements must be met.

I encourage anyone who is interested in becoming a home inspector to look into ASHI®; you'll be glad you did.

Home buyers should start their search for an inspector with ASHI® credentials and real estate professionals would be best served by recommending ASHI® inspectors. Hiring an ASHI® Certified Inspector is the best bet for getting a quality home inspection. But, even ASHI® inspectors are not all alike. Some have more experience than others.

Most veterans I know agree that field experience — actually performing home inspections — is the real way this business is learned. So, hire a person with a history of successful field work. In my opinion, a person who has done 1,000 fee-paid inspections is on his or her way to becoming accepted in the industry as a true experienced professional.

# An Ode by an Intrepid Home Inspector

An inspector's day can be long and weary,
  I work when it's hot and I work when it's dreary.

I climb up on high roofs; I crawl on my belly,
  I talk to the kids eating peanut butter and jelly.

I drag around a ladder and a case full of tools,
  I respect the sellers and all their house rules.

I spend time in attics whether it's cold or it's hot,
  I explain things to buyers whether they get it or not.

I peer into furnaces looking for rust,
  I peek in every corner but ignore all the dust.

I work hard at my job and take every action
  To ensure my clients' complete satisfaction.

I've been yelled at and cursed when someone's bubble I burst,
  Like finding a problem not apparent at first.

I've been chased and bitten, impaled and burned,
  Been exposed to stenches so bad my stomach turned.

I've inspected in sun, wind, rain and cold,
  Just like the postman whose story is told.

There were many days I wanted to call in sick,
  But there was no one to call; I was top kick.

I loved my job and hated it too,
  A feeling held by more than a few.

The people I met were for the most part great,
  Only a few were caught up in some miserable state.

In the end it was worth it; I was enriched by so much,
  Experience, friendships, helping people and such.

I'd do it again – the roofs, crawlspaces, attics and all,
  Hmmm, maybe my retirement is not quite so bad after all!


                                        Rudy Platzer

# THE DIARY

## A Thousand Points of Light

It was a blistering hot summer day in the middle of a protracted drought in our area. It had not rained for weeks. But as hot as it was, I reminded myself that it was better than inspecting houses on some of the bitterly cold, wet days of our Midwestern winters.

The seller of this 80-year old house was a real estate agent who bought it the year before, made some repairs and was turning it for a profit. The buyer was a young, first-time buyer who followed me through the entire inspection with great interest in every facet of the property.

Attics were usually one of the last things I inspected. Many times they are dirty places and in this old house especially, I didn't want to track coal soot on the new carpet. So, I grabbed my ladder and headed for the second story attic access hatch. The real estate agent/seller had told me the roof was new, and because I had already walked it, I certainly did not expect to see any roof problems from inside the attic.

I popped open the hatch and before I could reach for my flashlight, I saw the proverbial "thousand points of light." Small rays of sunshine entering across the entire roof field — an unexpected surprise. I had never seen anything like this before!

What happened? One possible scenario is that the agent/owner asked a roofing contractor for an estimate to replace the roof. The roofer probably told him that the roof had two layers of asphalt shingles installed over the original wood shingles. He no doubt explained that all three layers would need to be removed, wood sheathing and tar paper would have to be installed over the original open slats that supported the wood shingles, and then the new roof could be installed.

Perhaps the agent asked if he could skip the sheathing and tar paper to keep costs down. If the roofer was a professional, he likely said he could not. Then maybe the agent/owner called another roofer or perhaps "his handyman" and explained the situation. Ultimately someone agreed to skip the sheathing and tar paper. There certainly could have been other scenarios, but in any case this installation was critically flawed!

The tops of the shingles were drooping down behind the wood slats, creating the star-studded extravaganza above me. If it had been raining at the time, I might have instead been treated to a bath under the world's largest shower head!

**BOTTOM LINE: Even a "new" roof might not be a "good" roof. Roofs should always be inspected from both the top and from the attic.**

## The New Air Conditioner

It was an older house that had never been air conditioned. My client, the buyer, called my attention to the listing ad which featured a "new air conditioner!" Guess what? I couldn't find it — although I did notice an older condenser unit sitting in a child's wagon on the back porch.

My client was understandably disturbed by this, so I offered to call the listing agent to find out what was going on. She explained that the owner had not yet gotten around to installing the new air conditioner but would do it at once. I called her attention to the age of the condenser unit and she said, "Well, it is new in that the house had never had air conditioning." I then explained to her that the condensing unit was only a part of the system. The homeowner would also need to install a properly sized evaporator coil inside the furnace air handler which would require modification of the furnace cabinet. I also pointed out that the size of the electrical service would not support the additional air conditioner load. A larger electrical service would have to be installed, and new wiring would have to be run from the larger electric panel to both the inside and outside system components, along with refrigerant gas piping.

I couldn't resist asking her if the home owner was qualified to perform this installation and pointed out that he would have to take out a permit for the work, and that the work would be inspected by a local code inspector. There was a lengthy pause, followed by "Who is this again? What's your number, I'll get back to you."

Well, she didn't need to get back to me because I had no further role to play other than to offer to return at my client's request to inspect the air conditioning system if and when it was ever installed.

"No", he said," I'm no longer interested in this house." Could you blame him?

**BOTTOM LINE: There ain't nothing quite like truth in advertising!**

# A Long Story

A lawsuit against the builder of a large, expensive custom home proved to be a long, drawn out process. The litigation had been underway for two years before I became involved as an expert witness. (I learned later that the attorneys were not satisfied with the experts who had preceded me.) The case ran for another year prior to my courtroom testimony. (Incidentally, my testimony took two full days, for a total of 16 hours on the witness stand. And, by the way, we won.)

I will try to make a long story short. The house had a number of construction and safety issues. The owners moved out after having lived in their new house for only a few months. Their young child had become ill from the mold found growing inside the wall cavities. And this was just one of a number of major problems. My estimate of the corrective actions needed to make the house safe and habitable approached $500,000.

The builder claimed there was no construction standard to hold him to because there was no building code in that county. I testified that, written or unwritten, there was a standard to which he could be held — a standard of safety. I testified that if a contractor builds a house which is unsafe, he could be held accountable irrespective of any codes or even in the absence of codes.

Safe building practices have evolved over centuries and are generally accepted throughout the construction industry. And, it's interesting to note, that all building codes address one common denominator — safety. Therefore, written or unwritten, there is a basic safety standard which parallels the purpose for which minimum building standards are established. The jury had no trouble accepting and understanding this simple chain of logic but it took two long days of testimony and a number of legal gymnastics to get there.

**BOTTOM LINE: New houses can have serious problems, and builders cannot hide behind a lack of building codes. Every new house should be inspected during its construction by a professional home inspector.**

# Looks Can Be Deceiving

When I pulled up in front of the 30 year old ranch on a slab, the roof immediately caught my eye. The asphalt shingles were a light grey — almost white, and appeared to be newer. The arithmetic was right. Light colored shingles over a well-ventilated attic can last 25 years, so I assumed this would be a second roof — maybe under five years old.

After ascending to the top of my ladder, I recalled the old saying about assuming something. This was the original roof! Although the shingle field was nice and flat, they were badly worn and holed throughout. I could actually insert my ballpoint into the holes.

The out-of-state buyer had been unable to attend the inspection (I always recommend attendance) but the agent with whom I was working was there. I had my client's permission to discuss my findings with her, so I told her about the roof.

Her response was something just short of accusing me of being a liar, stupid or both. She was particularly incredulous because the appraiser "was just here yesterday and didn't even call for a roof inspection." (In my experience, many appraisers don't carry ladders.) I told her it was unfortunate that she couldn't see the roof as I did — from the top looking down, which incidentally is the only proper way to evaluate a roof. She asked if she could use my ladder to take a look, which I discouraged because of potential liability. She insisted, said she would be responsible, kicked off her high-fashion, high-heeled shoes and gingerly climbed the ladder.

Her only comment when she reached the top was "Oh my God!"

I asked her for the appraiser's number and immediately called him on my cell phone. I explained the situation and told him I was confident that he knew the roof was bad but just failed to note it in his report. He, of course, agreed that was the case and that he would amend his report.

The buyer got a new roof, the appraiser's reputation was saved, the real estate agent got another chance to "get up in the world" and I got paid. A good day!

**BOTTOM LINE: Looks can be deceiving. Never assume anything; inspect everything!**

# Just Like My Daddy Taught Me

"My daddy taught me to roof when I was 15 years old and I been doing it that way ever since." This was part of the testimony of the fifty-something year old witness on the stand. He was the roofing contractor who had installed the replacement roof which was the subject of the faulty workmanship claim.

I had received a call from the plaintiff's attorney asking me to investigate a purported roof problem in my expert witness role.

Upon arriving at the house, I immediately determined there was a serious problem — without even getting out of my car. The roof field looked like a roller coaster!

After inspecting the roof from both the top and inside the attic, I determined that just about everything that could be wrong was wrong with this installation.

First, the roofer installed the new roof over the existing two layers of shingles. Irrespective of any local codes, most roof structures won't safely tolerate the load of three layers — especially when combined with a heavy snow load. But the next departure from standard installation procedures was bizarre! To remedy the uneven surfaces of the existing shingles, the roofer nailed down a layer of ¼" plywood and then installed the new shingles over that. This was quicker, easier and less expensive than tearing off two layers of shingles — a win-win for everyone, right?

Well, ¼" plywood, more so than thicker plywood, is very prone to warping and that is what it did — creating the "rollercoaster" effect.

The general contractor who sold the roofing job hired this roofer as a sub-contractor. The general contractor was being sued and his subcontractor was testifying as to the quality of his work — which of course my testimony countered.

The general contractor lost the lawsuit. Based on his body language I doubt he knew enough about roofing to even understand why he lost. There are other stories throughout this book which address various potential problems that I've seen when people get involved with incompetent general contractors.

**BOTTOM LINE: Check out any general contractor with the Better Business Bureau. Ask how long they have been in business using their current name and in their current location. Find out if they have any unresolved complaints against them. Also, ask for a list of references. And be suspicious of overly glowing statements from past customers who sound more like they may be the contractor's family members or friends. Problems can arise when building or repairing houses. Competent contractors deal with them and avoid law suits.**

## The Scary Basement

I was inspecting an older wood-framed structure in an upscale neighborhood. The house was vacant. Later I learned that an unmarried school teacher had occupied the house her entire life. She was born in the house, inherited it from her parents and lived there until her death. As the story went, she lived alone and had a fear of the basement. That was borne out by the heavy-duty locks on the basement door. It was said that she never entered that "scary" place.

And was it ever scary! I have never seen more widespread termite damage. The wood floor framing was severally damaged. The beams, floor joists and sub-floor were all affected. This termite infestation had been raging for many years. That the house was still standing was a testament to the fact that houses of that era tended to be overbuilt.

The rest of the story will probably never be known. How could plumbers, furnace technicians and others, who must have been called in from time to time, not mention this situation? Or were they oblivious? Or did they alert her to the problem to no avail?

I drove by the place occasionally when in the neighborhood. The house was still standing and appeared to be occupied. Who bought it? (My clients didn't.) Was the disclosure in my report passed on to subsequent prospects? Was another home inspection performed? What kinds of repairs were made? Were the new occupants living "happily ever after?" Or do they also steer clear of the scary basement and live above it not knowing that the floors beneath them are being eaten away more and more every day?

**BOTTOM LINE: No part of a home should be ignored by its occupants. A neglected place might be harboring big problems!**

# Four Pages of Problems

A lawyer called and asked me to take a look at a new house. The young engineer who had it built had "four pages of defects that the builder was unresponsive to."

I went to the house, chatted briefly with the client and went to work. The house was not perfect to be sure. But then I've never seen a perfect house! The items on his 12-month warranty punch-list were all rather minor cosmetic issues. I told the client that while not perfect, the house would probably be "acceptable by contemporary workmanship standards." I explained that was how I viewed things headed for court. It would be unfair of me to participate in a case when I knew we would not be able to support the claims. He was very disappointed, saying he expected more for what the house cost. I explained that while I was sensitive to his concerns, I didn't think I could help.

Let me digress. I know from personal experience that contemporary building standards are often too low to satisfy some of us. When Ruth and I are building or remodeling a house I will often joke with her, "Let's not make it look *too* good; it won't look professional." To those who must rely on others to do their work, I sympathize if your high standards of workmanship are not met. I will probably even agree that the work could have been done better. However, this does not necessarily mean you would prevail in court. The acceptable level of quality has definitely been lowered over the years. But major defects are another matter. Defects which affect safety or habitability are actionable and should be pursued.

OK; back to the story. I asked the disappointed engineer if he wanted me to look around the rest of the house while I was there. He reluctantly agreed. (After all he was an engineer and he already knew what was wrong with the place.)

Because I had already walked through the living space, I asked to see the basement. It was approximately 30 feet wide by 60 feet long. The steel "I" beam running down the center length of the space immediately caught my eye.

I called to the client to join me.

I explained that the steel center beam which supported the floor and the entire inner structure of the house above was obviously ordered in four 15-foot lengths. This did not allow for properly extending the beam into the beam pockets at the ends of the poured concrete foundation. This shortage of at least 8" had been made up by extending the beams only about 1 ½" into the pockets, giving them insufficient support. In fact, the edges of the concrete in contact with the beams, was chipping off under the strain. Also, the beam had been "stretched" by leaving a gap between each of the four beam sections, rather than abutting them against each other. As a result, the ends of the beam sections were being supported only by the plates at the top of the supporting steel columns. These plates were not designed to carry this load and were bending downward under the weight of the beams and the floor structure above. Also, the beam sections were not mechanically fastened together, nor were they fastened to the columns. And the columns were not mechanically fastened to the floor.

I'll never forget the look on his face.

I told him that this grossly inadequate installation needed immediate attention. I underscored the stressed concrete that was chipping off in the beam pockets. I suggested he might want to consider calling his builder to demand immediate corrective action. He was newly concerned and also felt somewhat vindicated when I left.

**BOTTOM LINE: Even if you are an engineer and think you already know what is wrong with your house, there is no substitute for a competent home inspection. Home inspectors see things from a different perspective and as shown above, they**

have practical experience that allows them to see things that other professionals might miss. I have done pre-purchase inspections and defect analysis for a number of engineers, architects, real estate appraisers, and brokers who have recognized the value of my work.

# The Island House

I had advised my client, an attorney, on construction defect claims over the years and now he wanted me to inspect a house he was about to buy. His wife had found it and she was "absolutely in love with it."

It was a lovely house and had only a few minor issues that would be easily corrected. But one thing bothered me. I told the attorney that it appeared the house was built on a knoll and the surrounding land appeared to be low. Drainage provisions at the site appeared deficient and would be difficult to correct. I commented that during a heavy rain, the house would likely look like it was sitting on an island. And I recorded that observation in my report.

Two weeks later the attorney called me. He told me that, out of curiosity, the past weekend's heavy rainfall had prompted him and his wife to drive out and take a look at the property. They found that it was indeed surrounded by standing water. The "island house" was rejected and they were now looking for another property.

Fast forward. His wife found the same exact model for sale nearby and they wanted me to inspect it. It too, was a nicely maintained home but it also had a serious flaw. An added sunroom (which his wife "really loved") had a built-in structural problem and was at a point of near collapse. This was a large, expensive house and the sunroom was easily a six-figure project.

That evening I received a call from the owner, a prominent real estate broker in the area. He was quite upset and wanted me to know that his neighbor, a reputable custom home builder, had constructed the addition and he could not imagine that what I said about it could possibly be true.

I told him that my comments would be the same no matter who built the room addition. And, I explained that I always satisfy myself that my opinions are sound before reducing them to writing. I suggested that he pass my report along to his neighbor, the builder.

The next day he called to apologize. His neighbor came by to take a look and was embarrassed to admit that I was absolutely right. He was at a loss to understand how they could have made the mistake.

The builder called me. He let me know this was not the type of work his firm ordinarily did. He then asked if I had any ideas for correcting the problem without tearing down and rebuilding the addition. I offered a suggestion and he agreed that my approach would not only correct the mistake, it would also add an architectural accent consistent with the rest of the structure.

The work was completed. The structural change was aesthetically pleasing and the attorney's wife "loved it even more."

**BOTTOM LINE: The builder turned out to be a reputable professional who had made an honest mistake and corrected it. Moreover, the broker/owner used me to inspect all of his personal and investment properties over the ensuing years.**

# Warranty Contract Scam

I had inspected the house in the middle of the winter. It had central forced-air heat with an air conditioner. The furnace checked out fine but I didn't check the air conditioner due to the cold weather.

The next spring, I was called by my clients regarding a problem with the air conditioner. It seems they heard a loud "bang" when they turned it on for the first time and then the system shut down. I went to the house to take a look.

A one-year "home warranty" was offered with the purchase of this house so the first thing my client did was call the "warranty" company. They sent out a local heating and air conditioning contractor to take care of the problem. The technician who responded told them that the furnace/air conditioner was installed improperly and as a result it had a major malfunction. Since the improper installation was a pre-existing condition, the "warranty" would not cover it. But, the repair contractor could fix the installation problems for $700 and then the "warranty" company would pay for the damage to the unit — estimated at about $1000. Thus, he would save them around $300. And, of course, the deal was offered only because they were such nice people and he felt sorry for them and wanted to give them a break.

Well, guess who my clients were expecting to pay the $700 to correct the pre-existing problem which I should have found during my inspection? You guessed it, me!

I looked the equipment over and told my clients that it was installed in accordance with the manufacturer's installation instructions and the local code.

I also found the condition causing the "bang" and the subsequent shut down. As with all forced-air units such as this one, the fan is used to circulate warm air in the winter and cold air in the summer. The fan operated at a faster speed when the air conditioner was switched on because cold air is heavier than warm air and needs an extra push to circulate it throughout the house.

I reminded them that I had not switched the air conditioner on during my mid-winter inspection because running a cooling unit in cold weather can damage the equipment. When they started the air conditioner, the faster fan speed pushed a higher volume of air through the air distribution ductwork and a weak piece of the duct on the return air side collapsed and blocked the air flow — causing the unit to shut down. If a minor repair was made to the ductwork and the equipment reset, I felt quite sure the problem would be resolved. The cost would probably be between $125 and $150 and would be covered by the "warranty." The $700 and $1000 repair work? Yep, an obvious scam; I gave them a letter to that effect.

My clients called the repair contractor and told him they would give him another chance to look at the situation in light of my evaluation. They returned, apologizing for their mistake, and made the repairs according to my suggestions. The unit performed well, the "warranty" company paid the bill and my clients paid only the normal co-pay spelled out in the "warranty" contract.

Now, why do I continually use quotation marks when I use the word "Warranty?" The home "warranty" programs, with which I am familiar, are not really "warranties" in the strict sense of the word. They are actually more like "service contracts". This means that the "warranty" company will keep equipment in properly functioning condition for a specified period of time (usually one year) for a flat fee and co-pay. Typically, faulty equipment does not have to be replaced if it can be repaired and parts used for repairs need not be new according to the terms of the contract. All of this can be found in the small print and may vary from company to company.

---

Home "warranty" companies are glad to sign onto these contracts even though they have no clue as to the age or condition of the equipment covered. Experience tells them that repair and failure odds are on their side.

People ask me whether I recommend these service contracts. I tell them to read the entire contract. If the equipment covered in the contract is very old, I think they may be of some value.

**BOTTOM LINE: By all means know what any home "warranty" plan or service contract will and will not cover; then make an informed decision.**


# Blowing In the Wind

A thunderstorm was threatening as I arrived at the house, so I quickly put my ladder up and inspected the roof.

The house was twenty years old and obviously had the original roof. Although it looked pretty good from the street, it was badly worn and at the end of its useful life. I would recommend replacement in my report.

Upon entering the house, I picked up a copy of the listing which stated that the roof was "newer."

The seller was sitting at the kitchen table enjoying a beer (it was a hot day). He offered me one which I declined, of course.

I asked him how long he had owned the house. He replied, "About 15 years." Then I asked if he knew how old the roof was. He replied "four or five years." I let the answer slide because an inspector does not confront a seller. It's a good way to get thrown out of a house before your work is done — and this guy was big enough to do it!

But his answer raised questions. Did he really think the roof was only four or five years old? How many beers had he had? And why was the often used real estate sales term "newer" used to describe this roof in the first place?

My client was shocked when I told him the roof needed to be replaced. He had signed a contract to buy this place thinking the roof was "newer" and had been led to believe it would have years of useful life left. Controversy was beginning to blow in the wind.

I explained that I felt confident that any competent roofing contractor would agree with my evaluation. I suggested in my report that a replacement estimate be obtained from a reputable roofing contractor. This would give both he and the seller a second opinion and establish a price for negotiation purposes.

I told my client that I never like being the messenger of bad news but that it was a part of the job and had to be done. He thanked me for saving him from a bad roof that would have cost him several thousand dollars to replace. He would ask the seller to negotiate replacement as a condition for following through on the contract.

**BOTTOM LINE: Always determine how old that "newer" roof really is by having it inspected by a home inspector who walks roofs. Looking down on a roof is the best way to determine its true condition.**

---

# A Retirement Nightmare

The house was in litigation. It was a new, nicely designed, single story on a crawl space. The home this couple always dreamed of retiring to. Several months after they moved in, they discovered standing water in the crawl space. The builders would not address the problem, so they hired a contractor to install a drain system around the inside perimeter of the foundation. This directed the water into a sump, where it was discharged to the exterior by a sump pump. It proved successful in drying out the crawl space, but the soil under the foundation remained wet. Subsequently, things started happening in the living space. Cracks started to appear in the walls, door frames were deforming, and the floor was sinking. What in the world was happening? The builders had no answers and were providing no relief. Enter the attorney. He asked me to take a look.

The house was situated on a level lot and the living space floor was set at the existing grade level. However, it should have been set much higher to allow for a gradual slope in the finished grade around all four sides of the house. This would have facilitated drainage away from the structure and would also have created a separation of wood framing members from the surrounding soil. Because this important detail was missed, water was entering the crawl space.

When the crawl space was dried out an unforeseen secondary problem reared its ugly head. The expansive clay soil supporting the piers under the center beam floor support dried out and shrunk. The piers sank and the floor structure dropped down throughout the entire center of the house. The perimeter foundation, however, didn't settle because it remained wet .This was a classic example of what is termed "differential settlement".

What was the solution? Jack the house up, add at least two more courses of block to the concrete block foundation and correct the grading? Or wait until the piers stabilized and then raise the center beam and floor structure? Or perhaps install a drainage system around the outside of the foundation to dry out the soil under the foundation footings? These were just some immediate thoughts.

Home inspectors are expected to document their visual observations. They are not required to recommend corrective actions unless they feel qualified and comfortable in doing so. This situation would need the attention of professional specialists, probably geotechnical and structural engineers, perhaps others. But whatever corrective action was finally recommended, it would be an expensive fix.

The owners told me about the problem they were having with their builders. They were brothers who previously were heating and air conditioning technicians and aspired to be general contractors. (After all, how difficult could building a house be?) This was their first project. They gave the couple an attractive price and convinced them they would do a good job. Now, it appeared they were headed for bankruptcy.

These good people would be left holding the bag. Moreover, they lamented that they could not afford any large repair costs on their retirement income.

**BOTTOM LINE: Always check out a contractor thoroughly! Experience is key, along with testimonials from past customers. And, as always, check with the Better Business Bureau.**

# What Are You Doing On That Roof?

When the buyer engaged my services he mentioned that the roof was listed as "newer." As I rolled up in front of the house my compass told me it was south-facing. The front roof slope, which was readily visible, did indeed look newer.

I met my client, unloaded my ladder and mounted the roof. I quickly determined the shingles on the front of the house were likely less than five years old. Since this was the south slope, which gets year around sun, the north slope of the roof would show even less wear, I thought to myself. I went up and over the peak to view the rear portion. Wow! The shingles on the rear of the roof, which were not readily visible from the front of the house, were worn out and ready for replacement.

I don't like to cast aspersions, but I speculated the rear slope had several more years of life left when it became necessary to replace the more badly worn front slope. Then, after several more years the rear slope needed to be replaced. I would never, ever accuse anyone of replacing just the visible half of a roof. Never!

While I was on the roof, the listing agent drove up, got out of her Cadillac and yelled up to me, "What are you doing on that roof?" (Duh, don't all home inspectors always get on roofs?) I yelled down, "I'm inspecting it — both halves." After descending my ladder, the real estate agent approached me and asked how long I'd be. I explained that this type of house, in this age group, would take a minimum of three hours. And, depending upon what I might find, it could take longer. She very indignantly replied, "Well, I've never heard of such a thing!" I called her aside out of the earshot of my client, and calmly explained that I had made a deal with her broker. I wouldn't tell him how to sell houses and neither he nor his agents would tell me how to inspect houses. Her face turned beet red; she jumped into her caddy and left!

**BOTTOM LINE: If you're the seller, don't take any short cuts when repairing or replacing things in preparation for resale. And, if you're the buyer, don't use an inspector who takes short cuts, like not going up on the roof.**


# Those Annoying Drafts

I recently saw an ad on network TV for a $19.95 (get a second one for free – pay only shipping and handling!) strip of vinyl (similar to weather-stripping) to attach to the bottom of your bedroom doors to "stop those annoying drafts". Those annoying drafts — really?

The most popular type of heating and cooling equipment uses a fan to circulate warm (or cool) air throughout the living space. In bedrooms, where doors are most often used for privacy, a popular method for facilitating air flow back to a centrally located air return is under the door! I recommend those doors be undercut at least ¾" to provide this essential air flow if not done so previously.

This new TV gadget wants you to get rid of these "annoying drafts". If you do, these rooms will be effectively cut off from your heating and cooling system and will therefore be too hot in the summer and too cold in the winter.

**BOTTOM LINE: Don't believe everything you hear on television. Like many things in life, there may be another side of the story!**

# Two Different Views

The seller greeted me at the door and after a minute or two of polite weather talk, he handed me a home inspection report. The house was recently inspected for a buyer whose financing fell through. The seller was quite elated over the report declaring, "The house got a clean bill of health!" I thanked him, quickly flipped through the half-dozen pages and handed it back to him, replying, "Yes, it does look like a pretty clean report." He laid the report on a table, told me to make myself at home and left for a day at his office.

After making my way through the house and finding one area of concern after another, I took another look at the previous inspection report. None of these things were called out! My report would no doubt create a stir. Understandably, two inspectors with such divergent views would raise eyebrows.

I reviewed my write-ups to be sure I was describing things exactly as I saw them. I was convinced that I could stand behind everything I wrote but I wanted to be sure the problems were clearly described. The two reports were not at odds over differences in how we described problems, their nature or severity. The first inspector merely found no problems.

For example, the electrical system in this house was an absolute mess. The 60 amp service should have been reported as being below contemporary standards, and, as such, would not be eligible for FHA or VA loans. The main panel was a spider web of homeowner wiring and several subpanels had greatly overloaded the 60 amp capacity. Just about everything that could be wrong was wrong. Double-tapped fuses and breaker terminals, inappropriately sized fuses, breakers not matched to wire sizes, improper grounding at the sub-panels, and improper wiring practices such as a lack of cable clamps, exposed and unprotected wiring  and open box knock-outs. All of these problems were detailed in my report. This electrical system was overloaded and dangerous and that is how I described it. The previous inspector had made a single comment under the space on his form called "Electrical System" — "Well protected."

What the hell did that mean? It was beyond me to know what he could have possibly meant by that comment. It told me volumes about this "inspector". First and foremost, he had not performed the service owed his client. Was this due to a lack of knowledge or had he deliberately shoved the defects under the carpet? Either way, it saddens me to run across this type of situation because these so called "inspectors" give the entire profession a big black eye.

When lecturing at professional home inspection conferences I stress that an inspector's work is always subject to review by others. It is often said that our inspections are visual in nature. That is true! But, if you don't know what you are looking at you will not be able to call out problems!

I know some inspectors who don't remove electrical panel covers. This eliminates any chance of finding the many possible problems lurking inside. I remind my fellow inspectors that there are no short-cuts in this business and that lack of knowledge is not an excuse. We are getting paid to know!

Most inspectors are knowledgeable and diligent; I call them "professionals". But there are some who don't have the training, knowledge or experience to be practicing in this field; I call them "amateurs." These phony practitioners are a disgrace to themselves, the people who hire them and to the home inspection profession!

**BOTTOM LINE:  Be careful; hire only a knowledgeable and thorough professional.**

# A Minor Dispute

It was a windy fall day. I was there to perform a pre-drywall inspection on a large house under construction.

As I entered the house, I smelled a very strong sewer gas odor. I quickly checked a couple of sink drain lines and found they had no plugs in place. (When a plumber runs drain lines, prior to drywall and installation of fixtures, he caps them with plugs to prevent the escape of sewer gas.)

The wind blowing across the main plumbing vent above the roof was sucking sewer gas into the house. And sewer gas is combustible! I called the builder.

As it turned out, the builder and plumber were having a dispute and apparently the plumber went to the house and removed the drain line caps. After all they were "his" property. And if there was a chance he was not going to be paid, he had every right to retrieve "his" property. Right? But, did he have the right to create a potentially dangerous situation over a handful of plugs worth maybe $25? I don't think so!

**BOTTOM LINE: When people are involved in conflict they can become emotional and unreasonable. It happens all the time in everyday life. This plumber was definitely not thinking straight!**


# What is a Mastiff?

My knock at the front door was answered by the seller. I introduced myself and told him I would begin by inspecting the exterior and roof. He responded with something like, "Sure thing. Make yourself at home."

After looking over the front and sides of the house, I headed toward the rear yard, which was enclosed by a six-foot high privacy fence. I opened the gate, entered the yard and shut the gate behind me. (One of the important inspection protocols is, "Redo what you just undid" — open a gate, close the gate; open a door, close the door; close a switch; open the switch).

I took a few steps and just as I noticed the side garage door was open, an enormous animal came bursting out and headed for me at a gallop! It was too late to turn around and run. I would have ended up at the gate without a chance of getting through it. And with my backside facing the dog, a tender part of my anatomy would have become a bulls-eye! As he rounded the corner of the garage with grass flying, I crouched down, extended my arms and said, as calmly as I could, "Nice dog." The dog screeched to a halt in front of me and began trying to lick me to death.

The seller knew the giant dog was gentle but I didn't.

After that experience, I learned to always ask, "Are there any pets I should know about?"

**BOTTOM LINE: There's nothing quite like getting a slobbery bath from a giant Mastiff. To avoid an unnecessary panic attack, always ask about pets. If you are having anyone inspect (or perform work on) your home, be sure to mention your pets and their dispositions.**

# Bats!

I'll never forget this house. I approached the brick chimney as part of the second story roof inspection, pulled my flashlight from its holster, peered into the flue opening and was greeted by a dozen or more bats flying into my face. Luckily, none actually touched me as I instinctively jumped back. But, it gave new meaning to the word "startled." Luckily, as well, I didn't lose my footing and fall two stories to the ground. Those kinds of things do sometimes happen to home inspectors. It happened to me once!

About this time, the buyer appeared on the roof. I always discourage this for liability reasons. But he didn't ask; he just came up. I asked if he had seen the bats and he responded that he had. I recommended a screened rain cap to keep bats and rain out of the chimney. It could deter the entry of birds and raccoons as well.

Then he asked me about the roof. I told him it was about fifteen years old, with average wear for its age, and had about four to five years of remaining life. He said the roof looked to him like it needed to be replaced. I explained that I would have liked nothing more than to condemn the roof, if indeed it was worn out, so he could ask the seller for a new one. But, I had to be objective and fair. At this point he pulled a crisp $100 bill from his pocket and said, "The roof needs to be replaced now, doesn't it?" I tried to be gracious when I responded, "I couldn't call this roof worn out for $1,000. I wish I could, but it just doesn't work that way."

His expression turned to a combination of disappointment and embarrassment. He put the money in his pocket, we both turned in the direction of the ladder and I said, "The problem with those bats really needs to be taken care of!"

**BOTTOM LINE: A fair and objective inspector can't be bought. This helps both buyer and seller by rendering a report that can be trusted. And it helps build a reputation of fairness and trust for the inspector. And, if you are consistently uncompromising, you don't have to remember on which inspection you stretched a rule.**


# A Strange Odor

A client for whom I had done an inspection called me. He was not a happy camper. He told me about a terrible smell in his master bathroom. Now I've heard that bathrooms can become odorous from time to time but this sounded over the top. Because I was going to be about four blocks away on my afternoon inspection, I asked him if I could stop by and have a look (or a smell!). This seemed to have a somewhat calming effect and he eagerly agreed.

I remembered the house, of course. Large, upscale, newer, many amenities — including a large whirlpool tub for two. As we walked toward the master bath, I commented on the beautiful decorating and casually asked how they liked the luxurious whirlpool tub. He replied that they had not yet used it. They had been in the house for six months. Big clue!

Throughout our report booklet I provided homeowner information that many of my clients said was extremely valuable in helping them understand the workings of their house. One of the things discussed was smelly drain traps. When tubs, sinks and even toilets are not used for prolonged periods of time, the water in the drain line traps under these fixtures can dry up, leaving an opening through which sewer gas can escape into the living space.  I suggested periodically pouring a couple cups of water in any unused fixtures to keep their plumbing traps fresh and functional.  I wondered if this client had availed himself of this information.

We entered the bathroom and sure enough I smelled the pungent smell of sewer gas — it has a distinctive odor.  I leaned over the tub and put my nose near the drain to confirm the source of the smell.  I politely explained the cause and the remedy.  And because this was such a large house with only two occupants I suggested he periodically freshen all the unused traps throughout.

Ever smell sewer gas?  Nasty stuff!  And in concentrated amounts it can be dangerous.  Keep those traps fresh and live happily, and smell-free ever after!

**BOTTOM LINE:  Things are not always as they smell!**


# The Road to Hell

It was in the very early morning hours during a very heavy rainfall.  I received a call from a very distraught gentleman who exclaimed that his new home was flooded.  "Could I come at once to help him?" he pleaded.  I told him I'd come by first thing in the morning to take a look and see what might be the cause of the problem.  (I had developed somewhat of a reputation for analyzing basement water intrusion problems, hence the call.)

The first thing I noticed as I approached the address was that the house was sited at the base of a hill.  At the rear of the house, the view was of a number of back yards stretching to the top of the hill.  I pulled into the driveway where the occupants were carrying water soaked furniture and carpeting from the house. The homeowner approached me, exclaiming that he was going to sue the builder over this catastrophe.  We walked into the back yard together.

"Did you build the barbeque grill at the rear of the patio?" I asked.  He said, "Yes, I just finished it.  I didn't like the trench back there, so I filled it in and built the grill in that spot."  "Nice job." I remarked.  I then went on to explain that the "trench" was put there intentionally by the builder to direct surface water run-off from the back yards above to swales at either side of his house and then to the street and then on to the storm sewer.  We call these trenches "swales" and they are a necessary part of the drainage system on building sites such as this.  When he filled the swale at the rear of his house, the water came over the patio, entered under/around the garage overhead and passage doors and then down the stairs and  into the living space in the lower level. There was a long pause, while he processed the information. It was becoming clear to him that he had created the problem.

I explained that there was still ample room on his side of the lot line to restore the swale and preclude a recurrence.  Very little more was said; he was obviously embarrassed.  He wrote me a check for my services and I departed.

As I left, I was reminded of something my mother often said, "The road to Hell is paved with good intentions."  It was at least somewhat applicable to this situation.

Or as Yogi Berra would have said "It ain't what you don't know that gets you in trouble; it's what you know for sure that just ain't so".

**BOTTOM LINE: Before you change something, try to determine why it was done that way in the first place.**

# Free Furnace Inspection

I was called to look at a gas-fired, forced-air furnace. The caller had moved into town and purchased the house a year earlier and now found himself in a situation which made him "uncomfortable." He had had the furnace inspected by a heating and air conditioning contractor as part of his pre-purchase inspection. This was done at the recommendation of the real estate agent who told him the contractor was "reputable" and that "she used him quite often." He went on to explain that he had only recently heard about whole house inspections and me.

He explained his situation. The furnace had been given a clean bill of health by the contractor. Now, one year later, he'd received a card in the mail from the contractor stating that it was their policy to give prior inspection clients a free follow-on furnace inspection after one-year. He took advantage of their offer.

The contractor's technician responded, and in checking the furnace, found a crack in the heat exchanger. Without getting overly instructive or technically involved, suffice it to say that a cracked heat exchanger sounds the death knell for a furnace of this type.

The technician said that for safety reasons the furnace would have to be replaced and that as good luck would have it they were having a furnace sale. He could replace the furnace, in short order, for $3,000. "Just sign on the dotted line."

I looked at the heat exchanger. Some heat exchanger cracks are difficult to find but this one was huge and it jumped out at me as soon as I put my flashlight beam on it. It was not only a big crack, but also an old one. In my experience this crack could not have developed in one year's time.

What to do? I felt sorry for this person who had gotten really bad advice from his real estate agent. He had basically bought the farm on this one. I told him that none of my suspicions could be proven and that he did indeed need a new furnace. I suggested he shop around and check out all potential contractors with the Better Business Bureau. This guy was not very happy and neither was I.

**BOTTOM LINE: This was yet another obvious scam that unfortunately would be more costly to fight than the cost of a new furnace. What a shameful and costly lesson! In my opinion, an objective, professional home inspection by someone who is not selling anything is one way to protect yourself.**


# Retirement Dream Homes

A number of my new construction inspections have been for people who are about to retire. They are building "their dream home," and are excited about getting everything they've ever wanted in a house.

What's wrong with this picture? Very simply, they are looking backward instead of forward. And they may live to regret it.

Dream homes tend to reflect a collection of desires accumulated over the years – healthy, vibrant years. But, for most of us, the retirement years will bring at least a few changes in our life and our lifestyle. These changes can create new accommodation requirements.

For example, I have known retired folks who ended up not being able to stay in their two-story dream home because they could no longer walk the stairs. Had they thought ahead, they may have opted for a one-story plan or incorporated an elevator in their two-story plan. If a wheelchair becomes necessary, wider doors and hallways will pay off. Larger showers, with built-in seats and grab rails may no longer be just a luxury. Lever handles instead of round door knobs is a good idea for arthritic hands. Doors in toilet rooms which swing out allow a rescuer to open the door if someone passes out inside rather than having them slumped against an in-swinging door. Slightly lower light switches, thermostats and other equipment controls can come in handy. Installing telephones or panic buttons at key locations throughout the house, including bathrooms, is another good idea.

Many retirees will live on fixed incomes and so, with energy costs rising, the house should be as efficient as possible. Consider high efficiency furnaces, air conditioners and water heaters. Superior insulation throughout and high quality windows and doors can become "make or break" factors when it comes to staying affordably comfortable in a house over the course of a retirement. And we all want to live to be 100 and able to stay in our own homes, don't we?

These are just some of the things I've seen people miss in their retirement dream homes. I'm sure you can come up with others.

**BOTTOM LINE: If you are building your dream home, architects and good builders can help, but the key is your mindset. They tend to build what you want. Look ahead and think about what you might want down the road in your retirement dream home.**

# Termites Will Find the Leaks If You Don't

I have recounted in other parts of this book about how termites will go out of their way to find damp wood on which to feed.

I was inspecting a large and very old farmhouse, wood-framed with a large attic. While I don't look for termites, per se, I do look for damage which might have been caused by termites. Termite inspectors, on the other hand, point out damage but don't comment on the structural impact of the damage. Nor do they make repair recommendations. So it takes two of us to get the job done, unless you have a home inspector who is also a qualified termite inspector.

Back to the story, I had not observed any evidence of termite damage as I moved through the house but having entered the attic that suddenly changed. The wood framing at one gable end of the roof structure had been decimated by termites. There was enough leakage through the clapboard siding to keep the wood damp, making it a termite target. The lack of ventilation, not unusual in older houses, contributed to the conditions responsible for the attack. Termite damage in the attic? Yes, it does happen.

**BOTTOM LINE: Water intrusion is the demon that must be kept out of your house. There are many places through which it can enter; through the roof, through the siding, around windows and doors, through the foundation. Stay alert to signs of moisture and water and take corrective action as soon as possible.**

# Another Heat Exchanger Scam

I received a call from a past client whose house I had inspected a few months earlier. The furnace was older but functional and I had found nothing wrong with the heat exchanger. The client related to me that the pilot light had gone out and he could not re-light it. He called a heating and air conditioning contractor for help. A technician responded, looked at the furnace and told him he would be wasting money to repair it because it had a big hole in the heat exchanger. He then explained to him and his wife that the unit needed to be replaced immediately because it was dangerous and they could be overcome or killed by leaking carbon monoxide gas.

I asked my client if he had been there to observe the technician while he evaluated the furnace. He answered that he had; he wanted to learn how to keep the pilot light lit. I asked how the technician went about inspecting the heat exchanger. Did he look into the inside of the furnace with a mirror and a flashlight? Did he perform a flame test? Did he do a flue test? He replied, "No, he didn't do any of those things."

I cancelled my evening plans (not the first or last time) and headed for my client's house. I understood several things. First, a "large" hole would not have developed in the short time since I had done the inspection. Second, a "large" hole would not have escaped my attention. And third, no matter how "large" the hole, no one would be able to discover it without looking inside the furnace or using one of the tests mentioned above.

I arrived at the house, got out my tools and reminded the client how I had inspected the furnace the first time, walking through the process step by step. I let him and his wife both look inside and view the heat exchanger using my inspection mirror and flashlight. It was now becoming obvious to them that there was no large hole in this heat exchanger. Then I ran the furnace and explained to them the disturbing effect a large hole would have on the flame pattern coming off the burner. The flames were upright and unwavering just like, I explained, "rows of marching soldiers." I used an electronic gas detector to "sniff" above the heat exchanger after the burners lit and before the circulating fan came on; there was a negative reading. They were now convinced there was not even a small hole in their heat exchanger.

I went on to express what I thought the problem might be. I pointed out the thermocouple, a heat sensing device that protrudes into the pilot light flame. As long as it is kept warm by the flame, the furnace will function, given that all other components are performing normally. I advised them that failure of the thermocouple is common and that when it fails it no longer emits a "warm" signal and the furnace shuts down. And, I stressed that thermocouples are relatively inexpensive and easily replaced. But this possible malfunction was not even addressed by the furnace technician!

I told them, as I always do in these cases, they could believe whomever they chose to believe. I offered to write a letter outlining my inspection procedures and findings so they could present it to the contractor. I also told them that if they chose to replace the furnace I wanted the old one so it could be disassembled and further evaluated by other experts to conclusively rule out the existence of a hole in the heat exchanger.

They thanked me and I left at 10:30 PM. That's the last I heard of it.

**BOTTOM LINE: This time, I had an opportunity to check my work before the evidence was trashed. I saved my clients the unnecessary expense of a new furnace and their fears were allayed. Remember that a professional home inspector has no reason to stray from the facts; no new furnace to sell. If you have a question based upon a technician's finding, call the inspector back. I offered, in writing, free telephone consultation to all my clients for as long as they owned the**

house. I loved to hear from them; I loved helping them continue to navigate the shark infested waters of home ownership and repair. Life is good!

# A Contemporary "Frank Lloyd Wright" House

When I pulled up in front of the house, I was truly caught by surprise. This was a three-year old house inspired by the Frank Lloyd Wright style and it was beautiful! This would be a real treat to inspect.

The lady of the house greeted me and expressed her interest in helping me in any way possible; always a good way to start. Her husband was being unexpectedly transferred to a job that was too good to pass up and they were therefore selling their dream house — the one they had planned to live in after retirement. The house was soon to become a "third-party buyout" meaning that if the transferee couldn't sell it, the relocation company would buy it for his employer and then resell it.

At first blush I could not imagine that this house would not be very saleable. It was above average construction with a lot of amenities; it was well maintained and very nicely landscaped. But the transferee's wife offered their tale of woe; it seemed nobody was interested in this house. She said there had been several showings but not one single offer.

Why? This was their dream home; exactly what they wanted. But how many people were in the market for a custom house tailored to fit someone else's specific taste? This underscores a very important lesson: If you build a custom home exactly the way you want it, you may limit its appeal on resale. Sooner or later someone will share your taste in homes but many people won't. Another problem was that this neighborhood had contemporary homes with popular floor plans. This house was definitely out of place. We are a fad culture, pure and simple. People want what is "in" at the time.

Now I'm not suggesting you shouldn't build what you like. I'm just pointing out that we are all buyers and sellers at different points in time and if you want to plan ahead to future resale, you may want to consider what other people will want in the contemporary market within any given location. A sleek contemporary house won't be a good fit in a traditional neighborhood, and a log cabin or colonial won't blend in with ultra-modern homes.

Nice lady, nice house, but a design not very popular in the contemporary market. They had not even considered resale when they built because they did not plan to ever move. They were heart sick over leaving their dream home and even more upset over their inability to attract buyers. Things change; something to think about.

I might add that the one major problem I found with the house was a basement guest suite. It was a room advertised as a bedroom with ample closet space and an en-suite bath. Unfortunately, it did not have adequate secondary egress in case of fire. There was no window large enough for a fireman to enter with a survival pack strapped to his back. Building codes require a second way to exit a room built for use as sleeping quarters. How was this important detail missed by the architect or designer? Why was it missed by the builder? How did it pass the code inspection? Why did the real estate agent list it as a bedroom? Why should new houses be inspected by professional, independent home inspectors?

**BOTTOM LINE: Resale is always something to consider when building a house. All houses will change ownership at some point in time.**

# Termites and Kitchen Sinks

I have learned from experience that termites like damp wood as their first choice for sustenance. I often tell my clients that a good place to look for termites is under the kitchen sink, as this is one of the places in a house most likely to experience plumbing leaks over time.

I was inspecting a 150 year-old masonry constructed house in a downtown historic district, one of several such areas in my primary market. While inspecting the first floor structure from the basement, I noticed that some rather extensive repair work had been done to a number of floor joists damaged by an obvious termite attack. I also noted remnants of termite mud tunnels on the foundation walls which confirmed their visit. The damage was confined to the area under the kitchen sink cabinet; nothing surprising here. And, the repair work was sufficient. I was about to move on when I noted a termite tunnel in the flooring. It began at the repaired area and followed a space between two pieces of wood sub-flooring laid diagonally over the floor joists. I followed it across to the opposite wall. It ended its path at the exact spot where a corner of the brick chimney met the floor structure. At that point the tunnel took a vertical turn and disappeared through the floor.

At times I feel like a detective; putting clues together to reach conclusions. This was one of those days. It went like this. The kitchen sink leak was fixed; the termites were forced to look for another source of soft, wet wood on which to feed. They took the shortest, direct route straight to the chimney on the other side of the house. I had already observed amateurish tar patching at the chimney where it penetrated the slate roof. It was probably still leaking. What would I find upstairs?

Nothing on the first floor, but in the bedroom on the second floor my electronic moisture meter alerted me to dampness in the plaster wall abutting the chimney. My investigation was almost complete. Now, the coup de grace: I moved to the center of the room and lightly jumped on the floor. Not surprisingly, the floor bounced like a trampoline. The termites had made their way directly to the damp floor structure of the upper level, causing substantial hidden damage and yielding yet another data point on the behavior of these uncanny creatures.

**BOTTOM LINE: In my experience, only damp wood attracts termites so do what you need to do to keep the wood structure of your house dry. Insect instinct is an amazing phenomenon. If it suits their appetite, they'll find it. These tiny little white worms knew the shortest path to a new feeding ground in another, remote part of the house. Wow!**

# Is This Part of a Home Inspection?

One of the frequent criticisms I got from real estate agents was my focus on grading and drainage. I commented on low grading around foundations, improper roof water drainage systems, improper landscaping impeding good drainage, etc. Some of them looked at me like I had just stepped out of a space ship! How could these things possibly be included in a home inspection and how could they possibly affect the condition or habitability of a house? Let me answer by way of an example.

I was called by an attorney to provide expert witness testimony in a case involving a client who became seriously ill while asleep in his condo. The plaintiff had lived there for twenty years — since the development was new. He had returned home from a prolonged business trip on a "red-eye" flight and turned in for the night. Sometime later, he woke up struggling to breathe. He knew something was seriously wrong and he called 911.

He was rushed to the hospital, literally fighting for his life. He remained there for several days of diagnostic work and recovery. It was determined that he suffered a severe allergic reaction to mold.

An environmentalist, with whom I had worked over the years, was dispatched to the condo. He found a dangerous form of mold growing in the heating and air conditioning duct work beneath the concrete floor slab. The plaintiff was highly allergic to this mold without knowing it, as this was his first exposure.

Now, the question for me was, how did this mold suddenly appear after 20 years? I conducted a site visit. The answer was found in what had transpired at the condo complex while the plaintiff was gone. The condo association board of directors decided to replace the overgrown evergreens around all the buildings. They hired a landscape contractor who had pulled the bushes out of the ground, along with their root clusters, and replaced them with small bushes. In the process, the grade around the units' foundations was lowered. And, the concrete walks at the front of the buildings created a moat which trapped water. Moreover, there were no extensions on the roof gutter downspouts. They were dumping roof run-off directly into these lowered areas. The water ponded, saturated the soil, moved under the foundation footings and entered the ductwork. The mold followed. This formed the basis of my courtroom testimony.

The jury accepted the premise that deficient grading and drainage created the problem. The plaintiff won his million dollar lawsuit.

**BOTTOM LINE: Grading and drainage around a structure is indeed an important inspection element not to be missed during a professional inspection.**


# Goats Are So Cute

I was engaged to inspect a farm and the buyer wanted the barn inspected as well as the house. I completed the house inspection and asked the seller if it was okay to enter the barn. She said, "Yes, but we do have several goats. They are friendly but curious," she continued. "They should not pose a problem as they are corralled inside a fence in one corner of the barn."

I completed inspecting the barn structure, roof, electrical and plumbing components and then, because I like animals, I approached the goats. They all came to the fence and wanted some attention. One put his head through the fence and I petted him. He was so cute! Pets are wonderful! Just then I heard a crunch and felt a jerk at my side. Another goat had just taken a big bite out of my inspection report, which I was holding at my side.

Goats are very smart. One distracted me while another made my report his lunch. Can't you just hear it? "Hey, you distract this guy for me so I can eat his paperwork."

**BOTTOM LINE: Don't let a goat get your goat (or your report!)**

# The Rest of the Story

I was engaged to perform a series of progress inspections by a couple who wanted to ensure their dream home would be the best it could be. This was a large, custom home of unique design and their decision to have someone look over the builder's shoulder was a good one. I call custom homes "research and development" (R&D) houses because, by definition, they've never been built before and many of them seem to be problematic for builders.

The inspections were to be first of the foundation; then the framing, roof, windows, doors, rough plumbing and rough electrical prior to insulation and drywall; and then a third and final inspection just prior to closing.

The foundation inspection went well; pretty straight-forward — the foundation had been well executed. I was pleased for my clients, and for myself, and I was hopeful this was a prediction of good things to come.

Well, it wasn't to be. The pre-drywall inspection did not go well at all. I found serious structural, plumbing and electrical problems. I detailed these in my report and recommended my clients discuss them with the builder.

Since I hadn't heard anything from them after several weeks, I called to check on progress. They told me they had given my report to the builder. He informed them his "engineer" had looked it over and said, "Don't worry about these things, everything is okay." My clients then went on to relate what a good relationship they had developed with the builder, what a nice guy he was, and how pleased they were with him. They were also very pleased with his subcontractors who were also "very nice people."

I couldn't believe my ears! But then I remembered how bad builders tend to treat their customers like mushrooms — keep them in the dark and feed them horse manure!

I asked myself, "Why did they hire me in the first place?" I was perplexed and disappointed. I told them that I would rescind my bill for my previous work and would not be available to do the final inspection. Why? First, I didn't want my fingerprints on the house if the problems I found weren't resolved. Second, it was clear to me that they were listening to the builder and not to me. I was wasting my time and their money. I hated this because these were such lovely people and they really needed my help. But, they weren't responsive to my recommendations and so, under these circumstances, I no longer wanted to be connected with this project.

And now, back to the rest of the story. About a year later, these folks called and asked me to come by and look at some of the things going on in their house. The builder had gone bankrupt and they didn't know where to turn. I felt sorry about their predicament and agreed to meet them at the house. I must admit that I was somewhat curious.

Well, guess what? They were having problems in the areas called out in my report! The plumbing was leaking, ceilings were falling, electrical switches and fixtures didn't work, among other things. I advised them on how the problems could be corrected. It would be costly, and with the builder out of the picture, it would be at their expense. What a shame; such nice people.

**BOTTOM LINE: Didn't someone once say, "Nice people come in last?" Incompetent builders prey on nice people who don't stand up to them! And, if you hire a home inspector that you don't listen to, then your money would be better spent going out to dinner in a fancy restaurant.**

# What Are Those Shiny Spots?

The house was owned by a lay minister whose day-job employer was transferring him to a new location. It was a smaller, older house, but nice. The minister's wife greeted me at the front door and ushered me to the basement stairs. "Thank you," I said, "The basement is where I usually start."

She stopped in her tracks, "You're inspecting more than just the basement?" I said, "Yes, the order calls for a whole house inspection; I'll be looking at everything." "Everything?" she asked. "Yes, everything," I replied. At that she declared "Well, you can't do that today. We aren't ready for that today. You will have to come back later."

This happens occasionally when a lack of good communication somewhere along the line leaves people not knowing what to expect. And most people, though certainly not all, knowing that someone is going to walk through their entire house, look in every closet, under every sink, around every toilet, etc. will usually want to do some cleaning, move some things, or even hide some personal effects! So I told her to call the office to reschedule the inspection when she was ready — reassuring her that it was "No big deal."

It was a costly dry run. I had now lost an inspection time slot and accrued more than the usual travel expense to this remote location. We would have to do duplicate administrative work, and we would have to explain the delay to all parties involved. But, philosophically, this is just another one of the realities of running a small business!

Yes, there are many downsides in the imperfect small business world. You just get used to it and roll with the punches.

The inspection was rescheduled after about three weeks; that's a lot of cleaning!

I arrived at the house, and because a storm was approaching, I conducted the roof inspection first. The best description for this roof was, "worn out." It needed immediate replacement. In fact it was so bad that I told myself, "I'll be surprised if I don't find evidence of leakage inside this house."

I did my initial walk-through and the first thing I noticed was that all the ceilings had been freshly painted. I opened a couple of closet doors to find that the ceilings had not been painted, and they were full of leak stains! I tested a couple of them with my moisture meter; they were damp. Now you know *one* reason why I look in every closet.

I used my flashlight to inspect the ceilings throughout the house. Flat paint had been used, which is typical, but there were shiny spots here and there which reflected my light beam. I tested a couple of them; they were damp. The new paint was not dry in these areas because the ceiling had wet spots from the leakage.

I completed my whole house inspection, thanked the transferee's wife and left.

Among other things, my report recommended a new roof and whatever repairs the ceilings might need.

**BOTTOM LINE: Most anomalies are difficult to hide from a professional inspector. If that's your game then don't forget to paint the closet ceilings!**

**And, this was another lesson in humankind. Do not ever, <u>ever</u> rely solely on a seller to disclose problems! No matter who the sellers are and no matter what their profession! Always have a home inspection by a qualified professional home inspector.**

# The Poker Game

I had established a good business relationship with a client who invested in rental properties.  I had inspected a number of houses for him over the years.  He was a great guy and we worked well together.  He and his wife decided to build a new home and asked me to do progress inspections.

I found several problems with the foundation during the first inspection, which the builder corrected.  During the second, pre-drywall inspection, I found numerous problems.  I presented my report to the client and was shocked by his response, "How can this be?  This is a good builder!  This will slow progress and we need to move in!  You'll have to meet with the builder right away and get these issues resolved!"  I responded that my report was quite detailed and I would be more than willing to answer any questions the builder might have.  But I added that it was not within the scope of my job to supervise the construction, nor to recommend any specific remedial actions to the builder.

I went on to explain that there are architects who make themselves available to follow the work as construction progresses.  There are very few owners who avail themselves of this service because of the cost.  And, there have to be provisions in the contract with the builder to allow the architect to act with the owner's authority.  I reminded him that the inspection contract which he and I had signed contained no provisions for such supervision by me.  As an inspector, my concern was that problems be identified, but it was not my job to instruct on or supervise how they were to be corrected.

Suddenly, I was the bad guy.  My client was quite stressed, which is not uncommon for people building a house.  He was bombarded with the usual decisions of material and color options, plumbing and light fixtures, etc.  Now I had just dumped another batch of problems in his lap and he wanted me to resolve them.  I again asserted that I felt the proper course of action was for him to present my report to the builder and that I would be glad to answer the builder's questions.  Additionally, I would return to inspect the corrective actions taken.  But, I was not willing to interject myself between him and his builder beyond discussing my findings.  There might even be licensing and liability issues beyond my role as a home inspector.

I was hopeful he would understand.  He didn't.  He was upset and adamant.  It was almost as though I was the problem!  At that point I felt I had no choice but to end our relationship.  I told him I was sorry I couldn't be of further service and that there would be no charge for the work I had performed.

**BOTTOM LINE**:  "You've got to know when to hold 'em, and know when to fold 'em; know when to walk away and know when to run!"


# Cat on a Hot Roof

I like cats and cats can sense when people like them.  I was inspecting a farmhouse and throughout the process a farm cat followed me in lockstep.  It was almost embarrassing!  Did this cat think I was his mother?  On the other hand, the cat wasn't getting in my way so it wasn't a problem.

Well, it was time to mount the roof.  This was a 150 year old two-story brick monster with 10 foot ceilings so it would take every stretch of my extension ladder to get onto the roof.  I took the ladder off my roof rack and extended it to full length with just enough reach to make my ascent. I climbed the ladder, stepped onto the roof and began my inspection. Something was rubbing my leg — the cat!

Now I had a problem! While I was amazed that the cat had climbed the ladder, I realized that it would not be able to get back down without my help.

I finished the roof inspection and headed for the ladder. The cat followed me but would not get close enough to the edge of the roof for me to grab it for descent. So I got back up on the roof and tried to grab him; he was not having any of that. Now what? I went back to the ladder and pleaded with the cat. "Here kitty, kitty; here kitty, kitty." It was probably a funny scene, but not at the time. The cat finally gave in, came to me and I took us both safely to the ground.

**BOTTOM LINE: Leave those cats alone! Don't encourage a relationship with them. Get the inspection done and go home to your own cat! That's the way it should be.**

# Another Builder Bites the Dust

My client, a surgeon, was unable to attend the inspection, but said the builder of this very expensive "Homearama" house would meet me to discuss any issues I found.

The builder greeted me with the inevitable first question, "How long is this going to take?" "About three hours if everything goes smoothly," I said. I won't even try to describe his facial expression — suffice it to say he looked very annoyed! I went on to explain, "I'm not looking <u>for</u> anything, but I will be looking <u>at</u> everything. This is a large, complex house. It will take a minimum of three hours, so let's get started."

I explained that I would inspect the exterior first because some problems originate outside of the structure. Grading and drainage is always an important consideration, along with all the other elements — wall cladding, roof, roof drainage, windows, doors, decks, etc.

We exited through a rear door and I saw a serious grading problem. The back yard was beautifully landscaped, but the landscaper had created a rather large low area near the foundation. I explained that ponding water could result and cause foundation and/or basement water problems. He didn't come right out and call me stupid; he merely replied that the landscape contractor was competent and that he trusted him to do the job right. I responded that out of necessity, this situation would be reported as a major issue.

After looking at the rest of the exterior elements, we went back inside and headed for the unfinished basement. When I got to the bottom of the stairs, the first thing I noticed was the concrete slab floor — a large area near the rear foundation wall was cracked and heaved. I opined that water from the backyard had entered under the foundation and created hydrostatic pressure which forced the slab upward. Water staining around the cracks tended to support my thinking. In any case, I told the builder that I would recommend evaluation by a structural engineer and perhaps a geotechnical engineer to determine the exact cause and remedial action required. The builder did not respond; he turned, walked up the stairs and disappeared. I never saw him again. The rest of the house turned out to be in pretty good shape, but it took me over four hours "to look <u>at</u> everything."

**BOTTOM LINE: Some builders are open and in a learning mode: others already know everything they need to know. I've dealt with some of both kinds.**

# Termites Don't Eat Concrete

Termites are tiny subterranean insects. They live in underground colonies, much like ants. They feed on wood. There is much to know about these creatures; they are fascinating to watch and study. I mention some other personal eyewitness accounts in other parts of this book.

I am not an entomologist nor a termite inspector or exterminator, but as a professional home inspector I look at virtually everything visible as I work my way through a house. And I comment on the termite damage I see as it affects structure.

On this day, I was inspecting a post WWII concrete block structure, built on a concrete slab, with concrete block walls. The only wood structural element was the roof. By happenstance a recent termite inspection report was laying on the kitchen counter. It gave the house a clean bill of health.

During the course of the inspection, I saw what appeared to be a termite tunnel between a window opening in the concrete block wall and an un-caulked aluminum window frame. I made a mental note of this for use later because it made sense that this could be a path used by termites to reach the attic space above.

I couldn't believe what I saw upon entering the attic. Roof leakage had kept a large area of the roof structure damp over a period of time, attracting the largest termite infestation I had ever witnessed! There was so much damage to the wood roof and ceiling structural members that I immediately concluded it needed to be evaluated by a structural engineer.

My recommendation was followed and the engineer's report called for complete removal and replacement of the entire roof and ceiling structure! Remember that the termite inspector didn't find any evidence of termites? You should also know that I have never known a termite inspector who carries a ladder.

When evaluating professionals to inspect the home you are considering you might do well to hire a home inspector who, all other things being equal, is also licensed to perform termite inspections. And, make sure the person you choose carries a ladder and inspects attics!

And, for you homeowners, do go up into your attic occasionally and look around. Take a high-powered flashlight with you. If there is anything of a serious nature going on up there it will probably jump out and grab you.

**BOTTOM LINE: Problems can be lurking where least expected. Don't let your attic be an out-of-sight, out-of-mind trouble spot!**


# The Plants Were Beautiful

The call was from a concerned home owner who had a roof problem. His next door neighbor had told him that, looking from his upstairs window, it appeared the roof on his fairly new home had a huge depression in it.

When I arrived, I indeed noted a depression on the north side of the hip roof. What would be the cause? The first order of investigation would be the attic. As I wormed my way through the attic structure I found the damage. The sheathing in the plywood roof deck was rotted over a rather large area. Now I had to find the cause. I quickly ruled out a roof leak but I did observe a paucity of ventilation. And what was the source of all this moisture that was condensing on the roof deck and causing the rot?

I went into the living space and took some moisture readings on walls and ceilings. No elevated moisture readings were detected.

It was summertime. The patio and decks at the side and rear of the home were filled with a myriad of mature tropical plants. They were impressively beautiful. I asked the homeowner about how the plants were protected from our long, cold winters. He related that his wife brought them all in before the first frost. Ah Hah!

My conclusion was that the attic damage was caused by the plants. These large specimens consumed huge amounts of water and in turn released large amounts of water vapor into the air. This vapor moved through the ceiling and into the attic space where it condensed on the underside of the colder north slope of the roof. The attic was only marginally ventilated, and there wasn't enough air movement to move this large amount of moisture to the outside. Thus the condensation and the ensuing mold and rot.

My recommendation to the client was to increase the ventilation in the attic and drastically reduce the number of plants. This was met by a blank stare. I asked him if he had a question. He responded that his wife would remove him from the house before she would remove any of her plants! So be it. It would no doubt remain a continuing problem.

Oh well. We each have our own problems and priorities. In our house two types of plants are displayed — silk and plastic!

**BOTTOM LINE:  Don't solve a problem in a way that gives your wife an opportunity to choose between you and something she really loves!**


# It was a Gas

It was a beautiful, cool spring day. The seller answered the door and told me to make myself at home. She and her kids would be in the basement doing laundry.

As I started through the house I recognized a faint but unmistakable odor of natural gas. I immediately went to the basement door, opened it and as I descended the stairs the smell became stronger.

The lady of the house was ironing and the kids were playing on the floor nearby. I approached her and, as calmly as I could, told her that there was a dangerous gas leak and that she and her children should leave the house at once. I told her to leave the iron and the lights on (to lessen the chance of electrical sparking) and to leave the front door wide open as she left.

She complied. I then exited the back door, leaving it open for ventilation, and joined her in the front yard. I advised her to call the gas provider and report the problem. She complied immediately. I knew they would respond quickly to shut off the gas. They were there within minutes.

I asked myself how this could possibly happen. How could the strong odor of natural gas go unnoticed? Was it mistaken for some other odor? Had they just become used to the smell? I'll never know. In any case, a tragedy had been averted. I felt good about that. Yep, just another day in the life of an intrepid home inspector.

**BOTTOM LINE:  Natural gas leaks often go undetected and sometimes the results are disastrous.  We have all heard accounts of buildings filled with gas exploding when ignited by even the smallest spark or flame.  Never try to second guess a strange odor.  It could be something very serious and dangerous.  Get professional help at once!**

# There She Blows

It was a large home — older, good quality and basically well maintained. The original owner, and now seller, was there during the inspection; a very nice lady.

I was in the laundry room. There was an emergency overflow pan under the washer — good. When I popped up over the rear of the washer to view the plumbing supply line connections, voila! One of the washer hoses had a blister on it the size of an egg, ready to blow at any moment.

I found the owner in another part of the house and invited her back to the laundry room. (In our business it is professionally acceptable to converse with a property owner if there is a condition affecting safety or something that requires immediate attention.)

I explained that the rubber hoses supplied by the washer manufacturers are notorious for weakening over time and eventually bursting after several years of service. The results are nasty when they finally burst. A worst case results in a flood requiring new floor coverings, wall and trim repair and, if there is living space below, new ceilings, walls, and flooring. Sometimes it goes much further with damage to furniture and personal belongings — nasty indeed! And, of course, expensive! Even when it is covered by insurance, it is costly in terms of time and inconvenience.

I explained to the owner that she would be well advised to immediately turn off the supply valves to the washer. (Another rule of the business is never to leave your fingerprints on anything except owner operated devices such as thermostats and faucets. If you turn it on or turn it off and it explodes, implodes, floods, breaks, fails or falls apart you can wind up buying it.)

She shut the valves off and the day was saved; a great win-win for her, me and my clients.

I brought my clients into the laundry to explain the situation. (I think I found them in the living room measuring for drapes.) I explained the potential problem and went on to deliver my standard tutorial on this subject. It goes like this. First, an overflow pan can handle minor leaks and occasional overflows. But when a washer hose fails the pan cannot handle the gush of water. The drain under the pan is a gravity drain while the supply piping is under the water pressure necessary to provide sufficient water flow throughout the house. When a supply line breaks, all hell breaks loose — as in water everywhere! The water pressure in water supply lines in the average house is usually over 60 pounds per square inch. The flow coming from a breach in any supply line in the house could be compared to the water coming out of a garden hose at full force. This amount of water cannot be contained in an overflow pan — even if that pan is connected to the drainage system. Gravity drains cannot keep up with that kind of flow and a flood ensues.

To guard against this type of mishap:

1. Have an overflow pan to contain any minor leaks or overflows.

2. Install reinforced washer supply hoses available at home improvement stores. These hoses are sheathed in webbed stainless steel covers that prevent the problem blisters.

3. Shut off the washer supply valves when you are not using the washer and especially when you are gone for any length of time.

4. Have a water shut-off valve installed at the washer within easy reach which requires only one hand movement to turn it off. The problem with standard round handle shut-offs is that they are not handy and people are not prone to use them.

5. It's also a good idea to always shut the house water supply off at the main shut-off valve when you will be gone for a day or more. You should know where it is — ask your home inspector or plumber.

**BOTTOM LINE: An ounce of prevention…..**


# A Smell to Remember

An attorney called and asked me to take a look at a rural property. The recent homebuyers moved out shortly after taking occupancy because of a persistent, unpleasant odor throughout the house.

The house was not a traditional structure. I have no idea why, but it had a wood framed floor built over a concrete slab. The county in which the house was located has no building code, so "anything goes". (But then I wasn't there to evaluate structure; just the smell!)

The buyer met me and showed me through the house. There were "smell-goods" plugged into nearly every electrical receptacle. He said they were in place when they moved in. He had cut several openings in the floor to expose the slab below. The concrete was covered by dried matter; I could tell at a glance it was septic tank sludge. I questioned him and learned the material was actually wet when he first looked beneath the floor. I told him testing could be done by specialists to conclusively determine what the material was. I asked him if he had a septic inspection prior to closing. No, he had not had any inspections. The seller seemed like a nice guy and he believed him when he told him that everything was "Okay."

My sense was that the septic system had been backing up into the house, likely before he bought it. I recommended he have the septic system inspected by a local septic system specialist with a good reputation, as a first step in addressing the problem. Ideally, this person would be the contractor who had installed and/or serviced the system. He would have a good knowledge of the soil structure in the area and an understanding of the performance and problems encountered with systems installed in that locale.

He asked me what might be wrong with the system. I told him I would not speculate, but it could range from something relatively simple such as a blockage, to a major failure which would require replacing the entire system. It could get very expensive. I also advised him that the septic guy would probably have a good feel for whether or not this was a pre-existing condition. If that could be determined, then the legal case might begin to get legs.

I wrote a report to the attorney with my recommendations. He called to thank me and that was the last I heard on this matter. Hopefully, they got the situation resolved and I wouldn't have to make another court appearance. Testifying in court is always challenging and exciting, but the preparation can be exhausting. My focus is always on writing "bullet-proof" reports that get a settlement and negate the need for a trial. I have been very successful at that.

**BOTTOM LINE: "Shit Happens!"**

# E I- E I- OH!

It was a vacant relocation house; my first job of the day. I was told the transferee had already moved to her new work location, 75 miles away. As I used the lockbox to let myself in I saw that there was no furniture in the house. It's a good sign — the house is actually vacant. No surprises.

I started my usual preliminary walk-through in the basement, followed by the first floor and then I headed upstairs. Just as I stepped into the second floor hall from the top of the stairs, a bedroom door opened and a scantily clad woman stepped out into the hallway. She saw me and screamed "EEEEEEEEEEE!"

I was shocked, to say the least, and stammered, "I, I, I, am the home inspector." She let out another "EEEEEEEEEEE!" I held my inspection report clipboard up and repeated "I'm the home inspector." Her response was "OH!!!!!!!!", as she darted back into the bedroom.

She reappeared wearing a bathrobe. She explained that she had returned to her previous work location the day before to tie up some loose ends. Thinking this could take longer than expected, she came prepared to spend the night in her old house rather than driving back to her new home or getting a hotel room. The real estate agent never told her I was coming; after all she had moved! We exchanged apologies and laughed the matter off.

**BOTTOM LINE: Never, never, but never take for granted that a house is vacant! Ring the bell, knock loudly, open the door and yell several times, "Is anybody home?" It may help avoid an "E I- E I -OH" moment which might not have ended on such a jovial note. She might have had a gun!**


# What Does THAT Have To Do With A Home Inspection?

I was inspecting the exterior of a 1920s house when I smelled natural gas. What? Could there be a gas leak in the middle of the yard? I mused that an old service line coming in from the street could have corroded, creating a leak.

The sellers were not home but their listing agent was in attendance, so I told her what I suspected. She replied, "I don't smell a thing! And what does that have to do with a home inspection?" I explained that the gas service line was the responsibility of the property owner, that it could be costly to repair, and that it was an obligation to my client, the buyer, to include the suspected leak in my report. There was some mumbling about home inspectors always causing problems, which I ignored. I went on with the rest of my inspection.

A plumber subsequently did confirm the leak and the repairs were paid for by the seller, as it should have been. A professional home inspector knows who he is working for — the client who is paying for the inspection. Sometimes sellers and their agents may not like problems to be found because they can be costly to correct. But that's the way it works! Home inspectors don't create problems; they just find and report them.

**BOTTOM LINE: Professional home inspectors have a responsibility to one person only — their client!**

# Keeping the Air Fresh

It was a modest, single story, wood framed home in a rural setting. It had an attractive exterior which appeared well maintained. The sellers met me at the door and graciously ushered me in; a very nice, older couple.

Upon entering, I immediately sensed the unmistakable odor of air fresheners. As I walked from room to room performing my inspection, it appeared they had an air freshener plugged into every electrical receptacle. What was going on here?

As I popped up through the access hatch to inspect the attic, it looked like someone had painted everything black. Black mold covered every piece of wood framing and the underside of the roof deck; I had never seen anything like it! I would recommend evaluation and remediation by an environmental specialist in my report. But where on earth was all the moisture coming from to support this overwhelming mold growth?

I headed for the crawl space next. I donned my coveralls, pulled up the entry hatch and dropped to the dirt floor below. My shoes sank into the mud. Crawl spaces are supposed to be kept dry; this one was definitely not dry! It confirmed my suspicions; here was the source of the mold problem. The entire space was wet, and there was a trench down through the middle of the dirt floor. It was obvious that water literally ran in a stream under this house when it rained. I had already recommended some grading corrections on my tour of the exterior, but I had no idea the drainage problem was this bad.

There was some mold on the wood framing members but, amazingly, no wood rot. This was probably due to the older, dense framing lumber which is less prone to moisture absorption than today's lumber.

How does a crawl space problem end up rearing its ugly head in the attic? The extreme moisture was rising through the floor, traveling through the living space and entering the attic through the ceiling. There it was condensing on the cold wood surfaces. A lack of attic ventilation was also a big contributing factor; there was no air flow to move the moisture to the exterior.

What about the air fresheners? Well, I'm hired to find problems, not to make judgments on my fellow humans. But occasionally you just have to wonder, don't you? Was this a cover up? How could the sellers and the listing agent possibly not have been aware that a continuing odor was a sign that something needed to be investigated. This house must have reeked of a strong mold odor for a long time. And to me, the cover-up fragrance mixed with the mold smell was even more repugnant.

This episode underscores the value of a professional whole house inspection. A house is a system made up of many sub-systems. When the sub-systems are performing well, a house will perform well, but when one problem occurs, it can have a dramatic effect on other parts of the house. In this case, easily correctable grading deficiencies around the exterior caused the crawlspace water condition which in turn caused an unhealthy condition throughout the entire house.

**BOTTOM LINE: Some real estate agents recommend individual inspections by trades people — plumbers, roofers, electricians, etc. These individual inspections typically cost more in the aggregate and do not provide the benefits of a whole house inspection by a person who is a systems thinker. How the entire house works together is critically important! Maybe we should be known as "home systems specialists".**

# The LA Earthquake

Ruth and I were flying to an ASHI conference in San Diego and had a connecting flight in Dallas. Every television in the terminal was broadcasting the news of a major earthquake in Los Angeles. Our layover time was spent riveted to the coverage.

Upon settling in to our San Diego hotel, some hours later, we felt a jolt. The chandelier above the dinette table swung back and forth. We turned on the TV; it was an aftershock from the earthquake — almost 100 miles away. That was the beginning of one hell of an eye-opening experience.

We were finishing our business in San Diego when we got a call from the Red Cross emergency headquarters in LA. They had heard about a home inspectors' meeting in San Diego. "Could any of you please come up here to help us?" was their plea. Their emergency shelters were overflowing and they didn't have enough information to plan for temporary housing requirements. Basically, they needed to know how many housing units would have to be demolished and how many could be made habitable with minor repairs. And, the local building officials were overwhelmed by the vast number of properties needing inspections.

Ruth and I were among a number of veteran ASHI members who said, "Hell yes! We can help with that." We called our office to rearrange our work schedule, and called our airline. They were glad to rebook us so we could help and they even absorbed the re-booking charges. We called rental car agencies but none of them had cars. They were sold out because so many LA residents' cars were buried in the rubble. Finally, one agency manager said, "Hell, take my personal car!" We headed off to LA.

We entered the temporary Red Cross headquarters which was set up in an older, vacant office building. The scene reminded us of WWII footage of British command centers in underground London bunkers. So many people scurrying around, talking on phones, posting information on maps and charts, discussing situations and making decisions. Everything appeared to be well organized and under control.

We were ushered to the volunteer reception center and welcomed with open arms. What could they get us to eat? What were our accommodation requirements? Impressive! We were interviewed and given a list of properties to inspect. We were introduced to a volunteer who would be our driver. He was an off-duty firefighter who knew the area to which we were assigned. We received instructions, reporting materials and Red Cross credentials and headed out in a marked Red Cross vehicle.

We were assigned to inspect a series of large apartment buildings near Hollywood. Our driver took a "short cut" through downtown LA where most streets were cordoned off and ankle-deep in broken glass from high rise office structures. Unforgettable!

When we arrived at our destination, we found street after street blocked off as "no entry" zones and patrolled by roving police units. Residents were gathered at these locations, and to our surprise they became hostile toward us. Why? We were there to help! They were angry because they could not get in to collect clothes, personal items, or even their cars (many of which were trapped or destroyed in underground garages.) They were desperate and unwilling to accept that many of these buildings were too dangerous to enter until damage was assessed by folks like us. We pressed on.

We made structural assessments on one building after another. These were large, two-story, 12 unit luxury apartment buildings with lower level garages. Some had surprisingly little damage while others deserved the spray painted red "X" for demolition.

Interestingly enough, some of the ones that would survive would do so because of one construction detail that professional inspectors always look for — anchor bolts embedded into the top of foundations. These bolts mechanically attach the frame structure above to the foundation. If the foundation moves very quickly, the walls and floor structure, if built properly, can move also. Without these anchors, inertia will keep the wood structure in place while the foundation is moved out from under it. We found such situations where entire buildings were sitting several feet off their foundations. Amazing!

There were numerous other structural failures found, but for this book, suffice it to say we saw unbelievable destruction!

When we returned, I had an opportunity to take an ASHI seminar on earthquakes. I learned about the New Madrid fault which runs from somewhere near St Louis down to the Louisville area. It is compared to the San Andreas fault in California in terms of its destructive potential. The danger zone extends into southwestern Ohio. I would advise readers in that region to buy very inexpensive earthquake insurance as did I, following this enlightening experience.

**BOTTOM LINE: Neither pictorial nor personal accounts can adequately describe the massive and widespread destruction we witnessed in Los Angeles. Absolutely indescribable!**


# The House In A Hole

It was an older, brick veneered ranch built over a crawl space. As I pulled up in front of the place I knew it would be a problem. The surrounding land was all higher than this lot, creating a drainage problem. Moreover, there was no place lower in the area to drain the run-off. This house was built in a hole!

The first order of business would be to take a look inside the crawl space. The hatch was at the rear of the house, covered by a couple feet of snow. I got my folding shovel, cleared the snow away and opened the hatch. I was greeted by several feet of standing water!

My clients and the real estate agent arrived and I told them I could not inspect the house until the crawl space was pumped dry.

My clients understood, but asked if I would please walk through the house to see if there were any other obvious major problems. I agreed.

The house was vacant. We entered the living room through the front door. I immediately smelled the pungent odor of dry rot, that unmerciful fungus that "eats" and destroys damp wood! There was a room-sized rug on the floor. The exposed hardwood floors around the edges of the rug caught my attention; evidence of termite tunnels!

It was obvious that termites were eating the hardwood oak floor and occasionally their tunnels would come close enough to the top of the wood to cause small breaks in the surface. I pulled the rug back. Evidence of the infestation was widespread. This floor had been literally destroyed by termites. Moreover, even without seeing it, my experience told me the soft framing lumber in the floor structure below would be similarly damaged. My clients indicated they had seen enough. We went no further and departed the property. I charged the clients for my time spent on-site and told them I would apply that amount to the whole house inspection fee if they wanted me to return after the crawl space was pumped dry. I was never called to finish the inspection.

Interestingly, the real estate agent, who had referred me many times before, never did so again after this episode.

**BOTTOM LINE: Another example of a real estate agent shooting the messenger!**

# Dead on Arrival

Part of my practice involved inspecting houses for employee relocation firms. These companies are hired to manage the full range of activities associated with the movement of corporate employees from one location to another. Often times, when an employee is relocated, the company will buy his or her house if it doesn't sell within a certain timeframe. When this occurs, the relocation company usually has the house inspected so they know what they are buying on behalf of the employer. For liability reasons they don't want to pass problems along to the purchaser. And, they may ask the transferee to pay for any needed repairs. The inspector's job is to inspect the house and determine the scope and cost of any repair work needed.

On one such occasion the young engineer transferee greeted me at the door. He related that he and his wife had just bought the house two months earlier and he was now being transferred by his employer to a promotion at another location.

He handed me a report on the pre-purchase inspection performed on the house before he bought it and commented that the inspector "found nothing wrong." He explained that his real estate agent had arranged the inspection by the inspector "she always used."

What's wrong with this picture? Well, for openers, it's usually not a good idea to blindly use an inspector recommended by the real estate agent. Some agents don't like problems identified because that can slow down or even kill the sale. Also, remember that traditional real estate agents represent the seller, not the buyer, as discussed elsewhere in this book. So what type of inspectors do you think they might prefer to recommend? The type who don't find problems?

Now, back to the story: The $85,000 cute little starter home had $22,000 worth of serious problems which the relocation company asked the young engineer to fix!

I call a house like this "DOA — Dead On my Arrival." When I am teaching home inspection classes or mentoring people new to the business, I stress that they must be competent enough to avoid doing DOA inspections. I, or another professional home inspector, may soon be following in their footsteps. Results such as above can be embarrassing, and can potentially become costly liability issues.

I really felt sorry for the young couple who were naïve and blind-sighted to the problems in this house. They will know better next time.

**BOTTOM LINE: Be sure to hire the right inspector — experienced, objective, fair and reliable. And, not necessarily the one recommended by the real estate agent!**

# Inspecting the Inspector's Place

I like to tell the story of a personal experience I had with a home inspector. He was hired by a prospective buyer to inspect the office building I was selling.

I was purposefully not present for the inspection, but my scheduler was there to greet the inspector and witness the process. The feedback was interesting if not alarming. The inspector arrived in a late model BMW with magnetic signs on the doors. He had no ladders, no tools, and no flashlight! He owned the local franchise of a national inspection company. (The same national company had contacted me several years prior to see if I was interested in becoming a regional training manager. After requesting and reviewing

---

their training materials, I quickly decided I was not interested. It was 90% marketing and 10% technical; my view was that this was a formula for disaster.)

On the other hand, neither do a lot of fancy tools a good inspector make! But, at a minimum, the inspector should be able to see the high places and the dark places to perform a professional inspection.

Interestingly, but not surprisingly, this inspector was out of business in no time flat. Good for the profession!

**BOTTOM LINE: Again, not all home inspectors are created equal. Find out who you are hiring. And be sure they carry a ladder and a flashlight!**


# Sinking House

I was called by a frantic couple whose house "was going to China." They related that their lovely 35-year old tri-level seemed to have begun settling soon after they moved in. Large cracks had developed in the foyer floor. The stairs to the lower level were separating from the upper floor. The fireplace and chimney were pulling away from the structure. There were large cracks appearing in the walls. Wow! "What in the world was going on in this house?" I wondered.

When I arrived, I asked the couple if they had done any work on the house or grounds during their short occupancy. They commented that the only thing they had done was to correct a drainage problem around the exterior. A "landscaper" had advised that grass was not growing in a large area of the yard because the soil was saturated due to poor drainage. They took his advice and installed an underground drainage system — and yes indeed, the grass started growing!

This was a big clue. As I walked around the perimeter of the house, it became clear that the house had been built on a site somewhat lower than the surrounding terrain. Why wasn't it graded properly by the builder? Probably to save several large trees which were far older than the 35-year old home.

The picture was becoming clear. The grading was low for 35 years and the soil was always damp as a result. And now, with the addition of a drainage system, the soil was drying out. And, the soil in the area was expansive clay. This type of soil expands when wet and shrinks as it dries out. When the irrigation system was installed, the soil supporting the foundation dried out and shrunk, and the house settled, I reasoned. What to do?

I suggested that they might want to start watering around the foundation to keep the soil from drying anymore, perhaps establishing some short-term stability to the foundation. I also recommended they consult with a geotechnical engineer to help them come up with a long-term solution. I recommended an engineer I have had the privilege of working with on several foundation cases. The couple was dismayed and somewhat in denial but thanked me for my advice. I left hoping things would work out well for them.

One of the lessons I learned over the years is that new problems in older houses can develop when new owners make changes to the property or when their lifestyle changes create different demands on the house from those of the previous occupants.

**BOTTOM LINE: Everything going on in and around a house is connected. Professional home inspectors look at a house, it's siting and the surrounding land as a system where everything must work together to avoid problems.**

# Thank You Very Much

A Japanese executive had just arrived in a small nearby town to manage a Japanese automobile parts plant. He found a house he wanted to buy and I was recommended by a past client to inspect it for him.

I showed up early and did my usual neighborhood survey. Was the lay of the land sufficient for proper drainage? Did manhole covers signify the presence of sanitary and/or storm sewers? Were there any high voltage electrical transmission lines nearby? Were electrical service lines overhead or buried? Did the presence of gas meters indicate that natural gas service was available? Was this a neighborhood of custom homes or "cookie-cutter" production homes? Clues collected during this initial phase of the inspection can answer a lot of questions and set the stage for what's ahead.

By the way, arriving early is always good for another reason as well. Anytime you have to make an excuse for being late to an appointment, e.g. "I got bad directions" or "I got tied up in traffic", it's a bad way to start building confidence in your professionalism.

The house was vacant and I was not given the lock box code, which meant the real estate sales person wanted to be there to "officiate" at the inspection — at least at the beginning. In my imagination I heard the royal trumpets sounding as the real estate agent's Cadillac came around the corner. I was impressed with the car and wondered whether I would be just as impressed with its owner. He introduced himself and seemed to be an okay guy. He introduced me to his Japanese customer, whom he had chauffeured to the inspection in his luxury American made automobile.

The client had a name which I still cannot pronounce. Luckily he had been given a one-syllable American nickname, "Mike".

The real estate agent had some bad news. Mike, an engineer who did not speak more than a word or two of English, was very interested in all facets of this house as well as American construction practices in general. But, unfortunately his interpreter called in sick that morning. He and I were in for a few hours of show and tell accompanied by contemporaneously devised sign language!

Mike was amicable and obviously very bright. I invented all kinds of hand and body movements that day in an attempt to convey the functions of various components and any deficiencies I found. Thankfully it was not a bad house!

The inspection took longer than usual for the size, age and style of the home and I was meticulous to document everything in his written report. But, by the end of the day, I wondered whether he felt he had gotten much out of attending the inspection, and whether he was satisfied with the "information" and my service. I handed him my hand-crafted report and he handed me a pre-prepared check.

He then bowed from the waist and said in broken English, "Thank you very much!" I have only a shallow understanding of Japanese culture and customs but I instinctively bowed similarly and said, "Thank you very much!" He responded by repeating the procedure, as did I. This went on several times until he finally shook my hand and said "good-bye."

To an observer it might have looked like a dunking dodo bird contest but to me it was a great way to close out another new and interesting experience.

**BOTTOM LINE: Experiences such as this made my home inspection career interesting and satisfying. I helped a diversity of people from every walk of life and I learned a lot about people. And for the most part it was a positive experience!**

# Home Schooling?

My inspection order form said, "Owner out-of-town on house hunting trip." I rang the doorbell, retrieved the key from the lockbox, let myself in and twice shouted, "Anybody home?" This was my standard procedure, learned from a previous experience. There was no response.

The first thing I do when entering a house is a general survey. I walk through the house to familiarize myself with the layout, noting where the main electric panel, furnace, water heater and attic accesses are located. It also helps me get a feel for what's ahead of me in terms of difficulty and helps me judge how long the inspection will take.

I walked through the tri-level house, finally looking around the lower level. I casually opened one of the doors to quite an unexpected sight — a teenage couple in bed, cowering under a sheet, apparently terrified by thoughts of who I might be. Was it the police? Truant officer? Neighbor? Burglar? Mom or Dad? Who knows what was going through their minds! I quickly closed the door, stated who I was and said I would return another day. I called my office and asked my scheduler to reschedule the job as I "was running late and wouldn't be able to do it as planned."

Somehow I knew that when I returned on another day, these two kids would be in school. Not surprisingly, they were nowhere to be seen the next time around.

**BOTTOM LINE: You never know what you might find in a house! In twenty-five years of inspecting houses I've probably learned as much about human behavior as I have about houses. Some of it was good and some of it not so good. Fortunately, as I reflect on this, some of my fondest life memories are of the overwhelming majority of uplifting experiences I had while inspecting houses.**

# One Little Problem

It was a very nice, well-maintained, and very clean house; the type of house that is a joy to inspect. It was a two-story built on a concrete slab and I was finding nothing of any major consequence to report. Then I entered the kitchen. Again, everything was going quite well, when all of a sudden I saw it! The floor under the windowed bump-out in the breakfast nook along the rear wall had settled conspicuously.

There was a relatively large separation between the floor and the baseboard molding. My clients were shocked, since this had not been disclosed to them! It is difficult to believe that the sellers, being as meticulous as they were, hadn't noticed this problem. I offered some advice to my clients. This was not a structural issue and could be repaired by one of several methods. But, it would be somewhat costly. My sense is that at the end of the day the sellers paid to fix it, and were probably relieved that it hadn't turned out to be something monumental which would have killed the deal.

Of course this assumes they knew the problem was there and were afraid to disclose it — deciding instead to take their chances that it wouldn't be discovered. Yes, yes, and yes, probably.

**BOTTOM LINE: Even very nice people may overlook things when selling a house. Never take their disclosure, or lack thereof, as gospel. I know, I sound like a broken record, but I hope you are beginning to get the picture. Always have any house you're buying inspected by a qualified, professional home inspector.**

# Early Foundations

Today's concrete foundations are strong and durable compared to some of the ones constructed in the early 1900s. Poured concrete foundations were introduced soon after the turn of the twentieth century. They were made of concrete mixed on site and the quality of many of them tended to be very poor. Houses with these foundations warrant a close inspection. I was inspecting one such house.

The basement had been finished attractively. The foundation walls had been built out with wood framing and were insulated. As a result, I could not see the foundation.

I found a small door on a wall cavity which housed the main water shut-off valve. This provided a sample view of the foundation. The concrete surface was badly eroded. I took my long probe (similar to a screwdriver) and scratched the exposed aggregate (gravel). It readily dislodged from the mix and fell to the floor in large chunks. I put the point of my probe against the wall and pushed. I could actually insert it easily into the crumbling concrete! I stopped, because destructive testing beyond inserting a probe, goes well beyond the scope of a visual inspection.

It was clear that this portion of the foundation was inferior and I so advised my client. I explained that because I could see only one small area, I could not comment on the remainder. The paneling and insulation would have to be removed for a thorough evaluation and we left it at that.

**BOTTOM LINE: Although I didn't know for sure how the deal progressed beyond this point, I had a feeling the client bought the house anyway. I usually didn't get any feedback unless I inspected another house for my clients. And I never, ever, told a buyer not to buy a house. Instead, I gave them an objective, unemotional evaluation. Beyond that, the decision process belonged to them.**


# Winter Illness

It was a warm, early spring day. As I pulled up in front of the 20 year old house, it presented itself well. It looked to be very well-maintained; a pride of ownership was quite apparent.

The man of the house answered the door and we exchanged some small talk about the nice weather. I complimented him on the appearance of his house. He related that they had tried to keep it in good condition for the twenty years they had lived there — since it was new.

As I moved through the home, my initial assessment was borne out. It was impeccably maintained. I'd be home for dinner on-time for a change!

I was getting ready to perform my routine testing on the forced-air, natural gas furnace in the basement. There was an installation and maintenance record attached to the front of the furnace cabinet. The furnace was original — installed 20 years prior. Not surprisingly for this well maintained house, the installation contractor had made 20 yearly inspection entries on the maintenance record. Minor repairs had been made over the years and no major repairs were listed. As I started my inspection, I immediately saw that the flue connector pipe at the top of the furnace was disconnected. It had been lifted off and moved to the side of the furnace exhaust outlet. I wondered how or when this could have happened. Then I noticed that there had been no sheet metal screws used during the initial installation to secure the flue connector to the furnace! What? A serious installation deficiency made 20 years ago and ignored for 20 years?  Unbelievable!  I was incredulous!  This was a serious health hazard!  All of the furnace exhaust gas had been spewing into the living space and for how long I had no idea.

I went upstairs and found the owners and a teenage daughter sitting in the living room.  I asked if any of them had been ill during the winter.  The wife's eyes lit up as she said, "Why, yes, we've all been ill with respiratory problems the doctor was never able to diagnose."

I told them about the furnace problem and conjectured that it could have caused the problem.  Carbon monoxide is a waste product of natural gas combustion that can cause respiratory problems, and in large enough amounts even death.

The owners looked at each other in dismay.  The father became very upset, "How could this problem have been overlooked by this reputable contractor I have paid over the years to keep us safe?"  I had no answer, of course.

The point to be made here is that for the lack of three five-cent sheet metal screws, this family's health was put at risk.

I called out the lack of these screws as a major problem in my report.  I have been challenged by sellers and agents for writing up the lack of three screws as a major problem.  They called me a "nitpicker"; I called it "saving lives!"  The occupants of this house were lucky — they were all still alive!

**BOTTOM LINE: I felt good about having found this problem.  And real estate folks should be very guarded in their judgments on the work of home inspectors.  It's unfortunate and disappointing when people allow themselves to be critical out of a lack of knowledge.  Oh well, just another of life's lessons learned by an intrepid home inspector.**

# Know when to Walk Away

I was engaged to inspect a vacant multi-family investment property in an inner city neighborhood.  I picked up the key at the listing real estate office.

When I arrived, I wondered why a key was necessary.  The place was wide open and totally unsecured.  I entered and began my initial walk through to see what was ahead of me.  I couldn't believe the trash, the stench, and the overall foreboding of this place.  I increasingly knew I didn't want to be there but my continuing curiosity of the Americana experience beckoned me to press forward.  My imagination ran rampant.  As I walked through, I conjured up all kinds of activities that probably were occurring there after dark.  There was plenty of evidence.  Suddenly, I realized that I really did not belong there.  I might not even be alone!  What if I startled someone sleeping in a dark corner and he confronted me with a knife or gun?  I quickly and quietly went back to my truck, my heart skipping a beat or two.  I was afraid, and I'm intrepid!

I returned the key to the real estate office, called my client and relayed my feelings.  I told him if he really wanted this property inspected he could hire another inspector or hire an armed guard to accompany me.  There was a long pause.  "Thank you very much" he muttered.  That concluded our conversation.

**BOTTOM LINE:  This was early in my career.  It taught me to be more discriminating as to what properties I would agree to inspect sight unseen.  Personal safety is always of upmost importance.  Dead or seriously injured inspectors can't show up for their next appointment!**

## "Fragile"

Etymology: Middle French, from Latin *fragilis*.  Easily broken or destroyed.

It was a very old house that had recently had a complete make-over.
An old house with extensive rework always heightens my suspicions.

Every old house develops problems over time.  Some are minor and predictable while others are major, requiring restoration knowledge and techniques too scarce in today's construction industry.  For example, minor settlement cracks can be patched and usually are not structurally significant.  Major structural issues produce cracks that require remedial action beyond a surface repair.  A good inspector must be able to discern the difference!

Now, back to the story.  I did my initial walkthrough in the living space and saw no evidence of any major problems.  Then I headed for the basement.  Older houses really get interesting in the basement; sometimes very interesting because problems that can be covered over upstairs are harder to hide in the basement.   In fact many major problems in houses of all ages leave tell-tale clues in the basement, so this is often where forensic detective work begins.

Okay, this time I <u>will</u> go back to the story.  I'm checking out the stone foundation.  This type of construction consists of irregular shaped stones, laid using the mortar of the time, which is often inferior.  Nonetheless, most of these foundations remain functional.

Things were looking pretty good and then I saw it!  The installers of the new high efficiency furnace and central air conditioning system had to run electrical supply cables and refrigerant gas lines through the foundation. They were probably in a quandary as to how to accomplish this.  They were used to making holes in contemporary concrete foundations with power tools, none of which seemed up to this task. So they removed a stone and in the process loosened several others.  The more they fiddled with it, the worse it got.  Soon they had a gaping hole.  Well, they wanted a hole and now they had one!  They ran their lines and now faced a new challenge — how to get the irregular stones back in place. They did the best they could, but the end result left a lot to be desired. Some fairly major repair would be required to restore the integrity of the foundation.

Being conscientious, they didn't just want to just walk away from this mess.  They realized that this portion of the foundation was a collapse waiting to happen.  So, they took a can of international orange spray paint and wrote in very large letters across the wall "FRAGILE."

**BOTTOM LINE:  Some defects are easier to find than others, especially those marked "FRAGILE" in large orange letters!**


# A Comedy of Errors

The house was small, older and well maintained. The seller was a widow getting ready to move into an assisted living apartment.

I complemented her on the many plumbing, heating and air conditioning upgrades I was finding.  She said she tried to keep up with things and went on to recount that a newer air conditioner had recently caught fire and had to be replaced. My interest was piqued.

---

She said that the outdoor (compressor/condenser) unit literally burst into flames. She called 911 and the fire department responded and quelled the blaze. Her insurance took care of the damage and the same "wonderful" air conditioning people who had installed the failed unit returned and installed the replacement. They were such "nice boys."

I had already inspected the main breaker panel and had discovered that the breaker protecting the air conditioner was twice the proper size for this unit; a mistake commonly seen. This happens when an older, far less energy efficient, "energy hog" is replaced by a very efficient unit which uses far less electricity. But the installers sometime fail to swap out the old breaker with one of a lower rating. Yes, a fire just waiting to happen if the unit were to have an electrical overload malfunction.

The first installation was not protected by a properly sized breaker which caused the fire. The same installers replaced the unit in kind and made the same mistake. Another potential fire in the making!

**BOTTOM LINE: The first installation was improper, yet it passed the code inspection. It was destroyed by fire and the fire inspector apparently didn't accurately determine the cause. The insurance company paid the claim and authorized replacement, obviously without knowing the cause. The contractor repeated the faulty installation and it was once again signed off by the code inspector. Amazing comedy of errors, wasn't it?**

# Walk and Talk

A huge world-wide manufacturing company was headquartered in my market area and a new CEO was transferring in and found a house. The selling real estate agent called to schedule an inspection on this large, upscale property. My scheduler told her that I insisted the client attend the inspection so I could explain any findings, answer his questions, give him information and even offer some maintenance tips. The agent said, "Yes I know but this is the CEO of Xx Company." My scheduler told her that made no difference. "We inspect for doctors, lawyers, engineers and CEO's all the time. And they all attend." She called back and said he reluctantly agreed to attend.

It was a beautiful warm, fall afternoon. I pulled up in front of the house. There was a stretch limo, with a uniformed driver, sitting out front. I met the CEO, an engineer and a very engaging person. We hit it off immediately. We walked the house from one end to the other, up and down, inside and out. It was a huge home in very good shape and we had fun dissecting it. It had a few problems, which he readily understood once explained, and we discussed and agreed on appropriate corrective actions. What a great guy! I could understand why he was selected to head up this international company.

It is interesting to note that I inspected this house two additional times during my career for other clients. CEOs, it seems, come and go these days.

**BOTTOM LINE: If you are an inspector, encourage every client to attend the inspection. Otherwise, they have no idea what you did or did not do for them. If you are a client, take the time to attend your inspection. You will never have a better opportunity to learn about the house. If you are there, you will find that you get far more out of the process. And you may come away convinced that you got your money's worth, perhaps even a lot more!**

# The Keys to Success

It was a cold, dreary day in the middle of winter. The inspection was scheduled for 6 PM at a location 80 miles distant. The client said that the house was at the end of a remote country road and difficult to find, especially in the dark. And because this was pre-GPS, they would meet me at a gas station just off the interstate and I could follow them to the site.

It was indeed remote. We made numerous twists and turns and finally ended up on a gravel road. I was relieved they had not left me to my own devices to find this place. It was a great way to get the inspection started.

They had a key to the two story vacant house, built on a crawl space. We entered and I presented my contract for them to read and sign. I went to work and we moved rather quickly through the house, finding only some minor problems.

The last thing I inspected was the crawl space beneath the house. These places tend to be dirty, if not nasty, so I routinely saved this part until last. This part of the inspection went smoothly as well. I'd be home earlier than expected.

I completed their report, presented it, received payment and told them I'd retrace my steps back through the house to be sure everything was just as we'd found it. Lights off, doors locked, appliance and equipment controls returned to their original settings, etc.

Because I have developed a rather keen sense of retracing the route back from an inspection location and because it was getting late, I told them to go ahead. I felt confident I could find my way back to the highway. I wished them luck and they departed. I completed my usual double-checks, locked the front door behind me, loaded my ladders on my truck, and reached into my pocket for my keys. Oh no, they weren't there; nor in any other pocket! It's now 11 PM on a very dark, cold night and I am locked out and stranded!

My first reaction was to call Ruth on my cell phone. It would be an hour and a half before she could arrive with another set of keys. And how could she ever find the place? While I intuitively knew the return route, I couldn't explain it in reverse. She said she would call the clients for directions. She called back to report that she could not reach them but would begin driving in my general direction and keep trying them. I was getting cold and this situation seemed to be heading nowhere fast!

Suddenly, a pair of headlights appeared down the road and a car turned into the driveway. It was my clients, returning to retrieve something they had inadvertently left in the house. They were as surprised to see me as I was to see them!

We entered the house and I went directly to the crawl space. It was a tight crawl and not easy to traverse, but I went through it as quickly as possible. I found my keys on the floor in a far corner. I called Ruth with the good news. She headed back home and so did I.

The clients, realizing my plight, insisted upon leading me back out to the main highway, for which I was very appreciative. Getting lost would not have been a very good way to end the evening. When I got back to the interstate, I called Ruth and told her I was on my way; I'd arrive about 1 AM.

**BOTTOM LINE: Just another day in the life of an intrepid home inspector. Keep track of your tools and keep track of your keys! Make sure you have a well charged cell phone, and above all hope there's an understanding person like Ruth on the other end of your panic call!**

---

# Hawthorne Hill

By far, the most interesting house we ever inspected was the Wright Brothers mansion in Dayton, Ohio. The estate, called Hawthorne Hill, sits atop a hill in the affluent Dayton suburb of Oakwood. It was built between 1912 and 1915 by the famous fathers of powered flight, Orville and Wilbur Wright.

I'd often heard stories told about them in Dayton, where I was born and raised; I even graduated from Wilbur Wright High School. Little did I know that one day I would be privileged to inspect the grand structure I'd ridden by on my bike so many times as a kid.

As we drove up the long drive to the mansion, we were both excited and apprehensive — there would be so much to look at and so little time!

I'd asked for an early start time because my clients, for some unknown reason, wanted a finished report delivered to them that same day. Given the size and complexity of the structure, I knew it would be a very long day. I had recently inspected a nearby house of similar size and vintage which took me two 10-hour days. So I brought Ruth along to help on this one. As luck would have it, the full-time, on-site maintenance man offered to guide us through the mansion and lend a hand wherever he could. And, we were accompanied by an engineer, hired by the clients, to discuss our findings as we made our way through the property. He too, was willing to help and I put him to work whenever I found an opportunity. With this unexpected help, we were able to finish the site work by 7 PM, and turn our report in just before midnight.

The mansion was a masonry structure with stately porches and massive columns. The front and back elevations were identical and we learned later that Orville had designed the house and thought that each of the two brothers should have his own "front door". This symbolized the fact that they would share the house equally. Sadly, Wilbur died prior to its completion.

We learned almost as much about Orville and Wilbur that day as we did about the house. Midday, Amanda Wright Lane, great-grandniece of the Wright Brothers, came by to introduce herself and check on our progress. The house was being donated to a charitable foundation and she wanted it transferred in pristine condition. She volunteered about a half-hour of her time to relate stories she had learned from her father about the house. What a gracious and charming woman! And what a wonderful lesson on an important piece of American history!

I won't go into what we found in the way of defects; there were very few. The property had been meticulously maintained over the years. It was almost like inspecting a museum. The original furnishings and decorations were still in place. As we conducted our inspection room-by-room, we could visualize Orville sitting in his favorite chair in the library, tinkering in his workshop in the basement or using the circular shower he had designed to help soothe the arthritis pain, a reminder of his flying related injuries. Usually I concentrate on the systems and don't notice much else but this day was different. I have a vivid recall of every inch of that house and its features.

Describing this magnificent house in detail is beyond the scope of this book. If you would like to learn more about this historic landmark and view some pictures log onto http://www.daytonfoundation.org/hh1.html. Small guided tours are also now available at: http://www.escape.ovrpca.org/Events/HawthornHillTour/tabid/162/Default.aspx

**BOTTOM LINE: Even a well-built and meticulously maintained historic mansion can benefit from a professional home inspection. My hope is that the information we provided will help preserve this wonderful national treasure.**

# The Doctor Saved the Day

I was inspecting a house on a crawlspace for a young medical doctor. He was very interested in the home inspection process and was very attentive as we worked our way through the house. He took copious notes as I explained how things worked, offered maintenance tips and answered his many questions.

The crawlspace was always the last thing I inspected. Many times, after I emerged, I just wanted to pull off my dirty, sometimes muddy, coveralls and get home and under a shower as quickly as possible.

I told the doctor that because of the hostile environment he probably wouldn't want to accompany me on my jaunt through this crawl. I also pointed out that there was only minimum headroom and the journey would be difficult.

Au contraire! He did indeed want to accompany me. I went to my truck, got a pair of Tyvek coveralls, a face mask and a flashlight for him and we both entered the crawl. It was indeed nasty — dirty, somewhat muddy, a gazillion spider webs and a pungent odor that alerted me to the distinct possibility of finding dry rot in structural members. We would have to cover every square inch looking for problems.

About halfway through, we came upon a heating and air conditioning duct that virtually blocked access to the remaining space. It would certainly be in the best interest of my client, I thought, for me to complete this critical part of his inspection. I pondered whether I could possibly squeeze under this duct and I decided to try.

I have been known to do some heroic (dumb) things on my inspections trying to help my clients in every way I knew how. This would be one of those times. I got my head, arms and chest under the duct and realized I could go no further. When I tried to reverse my course, I found out that didn't work either! I called back to the doctor asking him to grab me by the ankles and pull. He obliged and with some significant effort he pulled me out. I didn't finish the crawlspace inspection but my client definitely knew I had tried!

I told him that if the seller would make some provision for entry, perhaps a hatch in a bedroom closet at the other end of the house, I would return to finish his inspection. I never heard back from him. I pulled off those filthy coveralls, went home to a hot shower and said a little prayer of thanks for the doctor being my "back-up" man that afternoon.

**BOTTOM LINE: You never know what you are going to run into. Being heroic (stupid) is probably never a good idea.**


# The End of the Lane

It was a long day and after dark. My last inspection was in a sparsely populated rural area. The house was at the end of a long, narrow gravel lane.

I arrived before my client, who arrived shortly thereafter. He parked his car behind my truck, walked briskly toward me and asked, "Do you remember me?" I told him he looked familiar but I couldn't place him. He responded. "I'm the guy whose house you inspected several weeks ago for a potential buyer. Remember? It was in the evening and you had been there a couple of hours when I returned from taking the kids out to dinner. I asked you what was taking so long and you told me your client had a lot of questions about the house. You told me you would schedule another time to come back and finish if this was inconvenient. And I told you to just get the thing done. Remember?" "Yes," I said. "Now I remember you."

He continued, "Well remember you said in your report that the roof needed to be replaced?" "Yes," I said. "And there were problems with the wiring in the main electrical panel?" "Yes." "And the grading around the foundation needed to be corrected and you pointed out several deferred maintenance items. Remember?" I said "Yes," in a somewhat quizzical tone.

He continued to relay to me that he had not taken my word for any of my findings. He had hired specialists to come out and prove me wrong. I was beginning to feel a tad bit uncomfortable. The punch line was coming and his car blocked my only route of retreat. Had he called me out to this vacant country house to get revenge?

"Well, guess what?" he said. "Everything you found was verified. That's when I decided I needed to hire you to look at the house we are buying. So, let's get started."

Some of the best compliments I received were when a seller from a previous inspection hired me to do the pre-purchase inspection on the house he was buying.

**BOTTOM LINE: I always tried very hard to be honest with myself, my clients and the other parties involved in a real estate transaction. This is the golden rule of the home inspection profession. And I slept well every night as a result.**

# Another Disappointment

I was selling a property that I owned and the buyer followed the recommendation of the real estate agent to use separate mechanical contractors instead of a whole house inspector. After all, "These are the technical people that really know what they are doing!"

The heating contractor found a hole in the heat exchanger and recommended a new furnace. His inspection report contained a proposal for a replacement furnace that the buyer could use as a negotiating tool. You can guess that I followed up on this recommendation by doing a routine inspection of the furnace. There was no hole! I called the real estate agent and told her that I would like to meet with the technician who had performed the inspection because I was having trouble locating the hole. I would most certainly pay for a new furnace to move the deal along if I could confirm the defect. Two of the contractor's employees responded. One had a pen light which he shined into the lower portion of the heat exchanger. I called his attention to the very dim light, so he sent his partner to a nearby drugstore for fresh batteries. He returned and we were ready to go.

He again shined his light into the heat exchanger and said, "See that dark spot, that's a hole." I said, "Really, that dark spot appears to be soot", and since it was within reach, I reached in and rubbed it clean. He then said, "It must have been further up." "Oh," I replied, "Let me get my long-handled inspection mirror so we can get a good look." I showed him how to hold the mirror and gave him my high-powered flashlight to look into the upper portion of the combustion chamber. He fumbled around and finally said, "Well, I guess I made a mistake." Indeed, and one which would have cost me $3,000!

I called the owner of the heating company and expressed my displeasure. I withhold an exact quote of what I told him to avoid an "R" rating on this book.

**BOTTOM LINE: Scams, scams, scams. After completing this book, I think you will agree they are out there. By contrast, professional home inspectors have nothing to sell but their expertise.**

# Have the Party on the Lawn

Wow!  What a beautiful location!  The house was situated on a peninsula extending into the lake.  And a beautiful house; looking good!  This would no doubt be a relatively easy inspection.

The house was built on a crawl space which I saved for last, as usual.  So far, the house was in good shape with many well-executed upgrades and only a few minor maintenance issues.  I was hopeful that the crawl would have no issues.

So, I donned my coveralls and dropped in though the access hatch to the crawl space.  Headroom was extremely close to the minimum 18" considered safe for traversing and I thought twice about crawling it.  But I nonetheless dropped to my belly and began.  Unfortunately, there was no plastic vapor barrier on the dirt floor which proved to be quite damp and even muddy in spots.  This created a humid environment which the spiders seemed to like, probably because they like bugs — huge bugs!  As I shined my flashlight around the space, the maze of spider webs appeared white in the reflected light — not unlike the kind we see in Halloween decorations!  Enough of that; suffice it to say, I was probably the first person down there in a very, very long time.

I concentrated on the wood framed floor structure because, under these damp conditions, you can expect mold and perhaps even dry rot (a form of mold that literally eats and destroys wood).  Well, you guessed it!  I found mold literally everywhere.  This crawl space definitely needed a vapor barrier!  And, the ventilation needed to be increased as well.  And, of course, the mold would have to be remediated.  I worked my way to the center of the house under the living room and my worst nightmare appeared above me; massive dry rot damage to the floor structure.  This would require some major repair work, complicated by the tight work space.  I crawled out, dragging the bad news behind me.

The surgeon who was buying the house could not attend the inspection but gave me permission to discuss the results with the seller and the real estate agents involved.  I would much rather have had him there but he was called upon to perform an emergency surgery early that day.

I headed to the center of the living room and gave the floor the highly technical "bounce test."  Sure enough it responded like a trampoline.  Why had I missed this when walking through the house?  Maybe it was the extra plush carpet.  Usually I can detect a soft floor, but in any case, I had (finally) found this one.

Up until this time I had been alone in the house with the permission of the sellers.  The seller and her listing agent arrived and I explained the problem.  The seller was aghast!  Her daughter's high school graduation party was scheduled for the next weekend.  I told her she needed to consider having the party outside on the lawn or at a different location.  Seriously, the floor was not ready for a crowd of jubilant graduates dancing the night away.  She was devastated.

The agent, a man twice my size in every dimension, asked me about the "bounce test" I had mentioned, and proceeded toward the center of the floor to see for himself.  "No!" I pleaded.  I didn't want him to prove how effective the bounce test could be.  He took the hint.

I never got feedback on whether the doctor went to closing or who fixed and paid for the defective floor structure.  It really was a nice house; with a major defect which needed to be corrected — no matter who lived there!

**BOTTOM LINE:  Really; never, never, never judge a book by its cover!  And make sure your inspector crawls every square foot of that creepy place down under.**

---

# What?  It's a Log Cabin?

In my practice, before every scheduled inspection, I received a datasheet from my scheduler.  It contained the date, appointment time, client's name and the address of the property along with a very brief description we used to determine the fee.  So I didn't fully know what to expect until I arrived at the property.  (Later, we used Google Earth to get a glimpse of the property beforehand.)

Routinely I would arrive, go about my business, get paid, depart and go to my next appointment.  But some properties were so unusual as to beg for additional information or explanation.  One such house was in a remote location, high on a hill.  It was a large, contemporary structure with a great view, but otherwise unremarkable.

It was a rainy day, so I decided to start inside, hoping the weather would clear up for the exterior inspection.  I had worked my way through most of the first floor and entered a room at the rear.  I was totally dumbfounded.  I was standing in the middle of a one-room log cabin, original in every respect.  It was as though I had just been transported back through a couple centuries in time.  And it was my job to inspect it!  And so I did.

I was alone in the house, so there was no one to ask about the history of this surprisingly uncommon structure.  But I knew the purchaser, a lawyer for whom I had done some legal investigations.  I queried him when I delivered the inspection report.  He told me the log cabin was built by an ancestor (as I recall, the grandfather) of Jonathon Winters, the famous comedian.  Over the years various owners had built several additions on to it, but they had all preserved the integrity of the historic log cabin.

Jonathon Winters is a native of the Dayton area.  He went to high school in Springfield, Ohio with my good friend Bob Circle, a popular area musician.  Both served during WWII.  They still converse from time to time.

Anyhow, Winters National Bank, now a part of JP Morgan Chase, was founded by Jonathon Winter's ancestor — Valentine Winters.  He may have been the one who built this log cabin.   Interesting, huh?

**BOTTOM LINE:  You never know what to expect; living history is always exciting!**


# The Spirit of Easter

A Jewish client, for whom I had done some previous work, found that Easter Sunday would be a convenient date for his inspection, as he had nothing else on his calendar.  And, the property was in an adjoining state!  I consulted Ruth.  The house was vacant, so it would move along quickly.  Ruth said the spiral sliced ham would only take an hour or so upon our return home for a late Easter dinner.  She would ride along.

We drove an hour and a half to the location.  It was a cold, rainy, bleak day.  Fortunately we had been given good directions and didn't have to waste additional time finding the place!  We met the client and completed the inspection.  He was happy and so were we, although wet, cold and tired.  After all, spreading happiness is a good way to spend an Easter Sunday, isn't it?

**BOTTOM LINE:  Ruth and I had spent the day together — and we had a joyful, albeit late, Easter dinner.  There is another point to be made here.  Other small business people will know what I'm talking about.  We made it a point to do whatever it took to satisfy our clients and to grow our business!  Even on Easter Sunday!**

# The Masonry Contractor's House

I've inspected a number of historic houses. If only they could talk, what stories they would tell! Occasionally, the seller would be present at the inspection to relate a story or two which had been passed on from one owner to another over the years.

This house was a beautiful limestone structure, circa 1870, with high ceilings, tall windows and doors and beautiful woodwork. It remained as elegant as the day the builder, a masonry contractor, moved in.

While walking up the curved stairway from the foyer to the second floor, I noticed an old and rather rough repair to the otherwise pristine walnut handrail.

The seller smiled as I stopped to ponder it. "Now that's a very interesting story," he exclaimed. He then went on to describe how the handrail came to be damaged and why neither he, nor any other of the previous owners had ever corrected the crude repair. During the great flood of 1913, this house, along with all others in the Great Miami River flood plain, was under water up to the second floor windows.

The mason kept his team of horses in the carriage house at the rear. He led them up the stairs to the second story of the house for their safety. The flank of one of the horses bumped the stair rail and broke it. It was a very interesting story indeed. And the rough wrought iron repair? Well, the builder was a mason, not a carpenter!

The attic of the house also contained an interesting surprise. The access hatch was at the top of a rear stairway. (Front and rear stairways were common in large houses of the day, the rear for use by the servants.) I carried an adjustable ladder for just such occasions but even after reaching the hatch, entry was a hassle. The opening was just large enough to squeeze through.

When I entered the space it was obvious that I was the first person in a very long time to do so. The floor over the ceiling joists was covered with a thick coating of coal soot and there wasn't a foot print in sight.

As I looked around, I made a startling discovery. The wood framed roof structure was grossly under built. The rafters were about half the size they should have been. It immediately raised a question as to how this roof structure had survived for 125 years without collapsing. Surely there had been heavy snow loads testing it over the years. Then it dawned on me; there was absolutely no insulation in the attic. The attic and roof deck were kept warm, allowing the snow to melt, thereby saving the structure.

How could such a spectacular house have such a deficient roof structure? A masonry contractor built the house, remember? He understood masonry construction, but apparently fell short on wood framing knowledge!

I recommended installation of attic insulation to my client but not until the structural problem was corrected by a competent framing contractor.

**BOTTOM LINE: Before making a modification to an older structure, the impact on other elements should always be considered. In this case, adding insulation without fixing the roof framing deficiency would have put the roof framing in serious peril.**

# The Handyman's Hidden Problem

It was midwinter and I was inspecting a house for a relocation company. The transferee was there during the inspection. He showed me around the house and was very proud of the remodeling he had personally accomplished. They had purchased the house about a year before and still had a copy of their pre-purchase home inspection report. He showed me the report, a clean bill of health!

I worked my way through the house, finding a few minor things, as I almost always do, but then I saw something shocking! The flue pipe connecting the older furnace and water heater to the chimney was disconnected and it was apparent to me that it had been that way for quite some time.

I called the transferee to the basement, took him behind the furnace and showed him my finding. He told me he had never been back there as he had no reason to do so.

I explained that this was a very dangerous situation. The older, inefficient furnace and water heater were putting their exhaust gas directly into the living space. And, the new windows and doors that he had installed had now tightened up the house so there was little or no air infiltration to dilute the exhaust gas.

Carbon Monoxide (CO), the "silent killer," is a by-product of natural gas combustion. And older gas-fired appliances tend to produce much more CO than newer, more efficient models. Unfortunately, this killer gas is odorless and can go undetected under otherwise normal conditions.

I advised him to vacate the premises at once and to get a heating contractor on the job as soon as possible.

He told me that his wife, who was resting upstairs, was eight months pregnant and had been ill for most of her pregnancy. He was understandably quite upset that his inspector did not find this problem.

An experienced professional home inspector doesn't look *for* anything. But, he or she looks *at* everything. The bad things just jump out and grab him or her. But, one must look at everything and have enough experience to get "grabbed." If you don't know and understand what's going on in any given house you can miss important issues. The previous home inspector had missed a big one!

**BOTTOM LINE: Real Estate Agents say, "Location, location, location." Concerning home inspectors, I say, "Experience, experience, experience."**


# The Repairs Have Been Completed

I was re-inspecting a house for a client. On my initial inspection I had called attention to several safety issues with the electrical system and she had asked the owners to have them fixed. When she was notified that the work had been completed she called and asked me to return to verify that the repairs were completed satisfactorily.

When I arrived, I found the paid invoice on the kitchen counter — $700 to "repair main electrical panel." The invoice was from a general contractor, not a licensed electrician.

I proceeded to the basement and removed the panel cover — and found that *none* of the repairs had been made.

My client was outraged and we both wondered who was scamming who! Certainly *someone* was not being honest here. What a way to sour a deal!

**BOTTOM LINE: If you ask the seller to repair something of a safety nature, it is a good idea to have your inspector verify that the completed repairs were done satisfactorily.**

# I Killed the Deal

It was a beautiful, early spring day.  The house was older and vacant.  At first glance it showed prolonged neglect.  I predicted it would have many deferred maintenance issues.

My client said it had been a rental, which resulted in its distressed condition.  He was interested in the house primarily because of its location, and he was willing and able to make necessary repairs at the right selling price.  He had hired me to help him make his repair list and to get a better idea of the cost of bringing the house back to a habitable condition.  We proceeded on that basis and I soon found that the water was turned off.  My client was surprised, as he had been told it would be turned on for the inspection.  It had been drained and winterized prior to the onset of winter.

I told him that it was important for us to inspect the plumbing system after it had been on for a day or two because if any water had remained in the pipes over the winter it could have frozen, causing serious problems.  If such a pipe were inside a wall cavity or ceiling, it could cause extensive collateral damage.  I was trying to be instructive, not overly alarming.  Very simply, the water would have to be turned on for me to help him achieve his goals.  I told him I would return at the expense of only an additional trip charge after the water had been turned on.  And, I suggested that it should be at the seller's expense since it was not a problem created by either him or me.  He told me he would call the seller's agent and get back to me.  We finished the remainder of the inspection and I departed.

A couple of weeks later my client called me.  He had presented my incomplete report to the seller's agent and asked that they turn on the water so the deal could move forward.  The seller reacted by attacking my report and said she would NOT turn the water on.  My client then asked for the return of his escrow money.  After several days of explaining the situation to the seller's agent and finally the broker, his money was returned.

See how easy it is for an inspector to kill a deal?  Here was a situation where a serious, qualified buyer wanted to purchase and rehab a distressed house and was taking a very smart, rational approach to doing so.  He was met by an unreasonable seller and her agent who were emotional rather than rational.  They chose to fight instead of resolving the issues and moving forward to closing the deal.

When I heard through the grapevine that I had killed this deal, I said to myself, "Yeah, right.  Sure I did!"

**BOTTOM LINE:  Legitimate problems found by home inspectors don't kill deals, but unreasonable sellers who may not be getting good advice from their real estate folks can.**


# It Was Electrifying

I was inspecting a "Do-it-Yourself" dream home with many built-in problems.  I found things like receptacles with open grounds (not grounded) and reversed polarity (hot and neutral wires reversed) and unprotected wiring in closets — all of which pose shock and electrocution hazards.  I was getting a clue that this do-it-yourselfer was in the dark on safe wiring practices.

The electrical system is arguably the most important part of a home inspection. All wiring and electrical devices must be installed properly for the sake of personal and fire safety.

I knew I would probably find many things wrong with the electrical panel but I was still not prepared for what I actually did find.

Curiously, I could not locate the panel and had to ask the owner where it was. "Oh, it's outside in a closet on the back porch." was the unexpected answer. Followed by, "My husband upgraded all the wiring and installed a new panel with circuit breakers!"

As I rounded the side yard to the back porch in a pouring rain, I noticed the electric meter swinging in the wind. The service entrance cable was attached too low to the side of the house, there was no drip loop and the meter was not even attached to the house — all grossly amateur work. Sure enough, beside the two refrigerators on the open back porch was an old wooden door. "This must be the electrical closet," I mused.

I opened the door, switched on my flashlight and was stopped dead in my tracks. I dared not even go into this room with my rain drenched clothes! There were wires everywhere! The panel cover (which I always remove to look for things like proper wire-sizes and breaker sizes and a host of other safety issues) was lying on the floor in a corner. The breakers were actually wired from the front of the panel, rather than using the knockouts on the sides, top and bottom of the box — rendering it impossible to attach the cover! This "upgrade" was a total disaster.

But, all of the lights and appliances worked, didn't they? So what was the big deal? Amateur electricians often use this "it works" test to evaluate their job. If everything works, it must be okay. The truth is, some of the most unsafe of all electrical installations "work." Their safety may not be tested until under the worst of certain conditions; then the house may burn down or someone may be electrocuted.

**BOTTOM LINE: Installing an electrical system is serious business, requiring the skills of a knowledgeable person.**

# The End of the Line

From time to time along the way, I was called upon to inspect a funeral home. I dare say, I'm probably among a very few people to ever have had the experience of looking through every nook and cranny of this kind of establishment.

Most people relate to the parlor sections or viewing rooms of these places, so there's no point my describing those rooms. But, what's in the basement (or another part of the building or even another building out back) was not only unfamiliar to me but somewhat shocking on my first time through. The specialized equipment, plumbing and appliances were straightforward as far as my inspection work was concerned. Plumbing rules are plumbing rules, after all. But my mind began thinking about how this equipment was used! Interestingly, I was never accompanied by anyone while doing these inspections, and was therefore left alone in these preparation rooms. They were clean, silent and somber. And, I must add, a bit spooky. I did my work and left — each time with a strange feeling of having been in the company of departed souls. I still think about it from time to time.

**BOTTOM LINE: Another lasting memory riveted in the mind of an intrepid home inspector.**

# The Amish Electrical System

  The house was an older two story farmhouse which presented itself well as I drove up. I instinctively knew it would be interesting day.

  The owner greeted me and was anxious to tell me about her house. It was recently remodeled by Amish craftsmen and she was extremely proud of the results.

  I'm familiar with Amish work in Ohio. There are indeed some fine Amish craftsmen, while some others don't deserve the title. Not too different from trades people at large these days.

  I was impressed by most of what I saw on my initial walk through. There were quality materials, quality fixtures, and very nicely finished carpentry. I also noticed several electrical sub-panels; I would inspect them later. I went to the garage where I found the 200-amp main electrical panel. I removed the panel box cover and immediately saw a glaring safety problem. The sub-panels were spliced into the incoming main service cable ahead of the main 200-amp breaker. To those of you unfamiliar with safe wiring practices suffice it to say this is a major fire hazard. There were also a number of other problems in the panel.

  I then retraced my steps to the sub-panels. As I recall, there were three, each of 100-amp capacity. None were properly grounded. And again, there were many other problems.

  I then gave the wiring throughout the house close scrutiny and found more problems. This was definitely an amateur job. And since this rural area had no building code, nothing had been subjected to a code inspection. I gave the rest of the house high marks but had to give the electrical system a very disappointing evaluation. Remedial action would be expensive.

  That night over dinner, Ruth asked how the day's inspections went. I told her about the nice Amish remodel with the bad electrical system. "Not surprising", she casually remarked, "The Amish don't use electricity in their houses." Suddenly it made sense to me!

**BOTTOM LINE: Electrical work is best left to professional electricians, not to those who don't believe in it!**


# A "Steel" of a House

  I have inspected many older houses; some with history worthy of mention. This particular structure was built in the early 1930s for the then president of Armco Steel. This corporation is still in business and continues to produce specialty steels in Middletown, Ohio. Remarkably, the house remained very much in its original condition. Going through it was like visiting a museum!

  The structure was of institutional quality and remained intact in every respect. Many of the structural members were steel. However, there was no insulation. And the original heating system was functional but would be grossly inefficient compared to contemporary standards. And, it would be very expensive to operate. In fact I explained to my attorney client, that energy saving upgrades would be a good investment as they would quickly pay for themselves in lowered energy costs.

Everything in the house was top quality in its time. The cabinets in the massive kitchen were made of signature steel and were still in pristine condition. There was also a large steel laundry chute which went to the basement laundry where still more steel cabinets and steel folding tables abounded.

The formal dining room housed a table to seat 16 or so people and had no doubt been used to entertain some notable dignitaries in its day. There was a foot pedal located under the host's chair so he could discretely summon the wait staff. There was also a pull cord on the wall behind the chair which would summon the live-in butler from his quarters upstairs at the rear of the house.

In addition, every room in the house had an intercom station. The system consisted of tubes placed inside the walls which were run back to the kitchen and servant's quarters. The owners could belly up and talk into the mouthpiece with the message being distinctly transmitted through the tubes. I reported the system as "functional."

The huge master bedroom featured his and her bathrooms which were quite ornate. It also had large his and her walk-in closets and the adjoining sitting room contained a majestic fireplace, one of many in the mansion.

The largest of several guest rooms had French doors, leading to a private balcony which overlooked the grounds of the estate. What a treat it must have been to be invited to stay there!

**BOTTOM LINE: As a rule the things that I remember about any given property are the things that bear my scrutiny — the structure, mechanical equipment, roof, grading, etc. But in a house like this, it was impossible to ignore such unusual features. I think you can understand why I really loved this work!**


# The Cat was out of the Bag

There was no mention of a cat on my datasheet! I always liked to know if an animal was in the house so I could take special precautions.

When I entered the walk-out basement, there was a cat lying on a chair near the rear door. I like cats but this one did not appear to be friendly. So, I thought, "I'll leave you alone if you leave me alone" and went on about my business. I soon needed a tool from my truck. It might have been a moisture meter, an amprobe, a level or whatever — I don't remember. I decided to take a short-cut, out the rear basement door, to my vehicle. As soon as I opened the door, the cat shot by me like a rocket. Now what?

Once outside, the cat sat down and peered at me as if to say, "You idiot, you were an easy target for me!"

I approached the cat; we had eye contact and he was standing his ground. I lunged and grabbed him and the fight was on. He sunk all of his claws and his teeth into both of my hands and held on. I literally had to shake him hard to get him to loosen his grip. Finally, after what seemed like an eternity, he fell away and then quickly ran off.

I went back into the basement, made my way to the laundry room and poured liquid bleach on my bleeding hands. I still have scars!

I had the owner's office phone number on my datasheet so I called him to apologize for inadvertently letting the cat out. He said, "Oh, that's okay, he goes out all the time." Boy, how I wished I had known that earlier!

**BOTTOM LINE: It is a good idea to get as much information as possible up front.**

# Why Me?

This was definitely a "why me" house. It was immediately obvious that it had been vacant for some time and was in an advanced state of neglect. I would be at this address for a very long time. Why me?

It was a huge, two-story, wood framed structure probably built between 1870 and 1880. The clients were interested in it for its historic value. He was a historian working at a very popular local museum. She was the daughter of an old friend and fellow inspector, now deceased.

We entered the house. Oh my, it was even worse than I expected! Falling plaster, badly damaged floors, rotting window frames. Ancient plumbing, heating and electrical systems, all of which would have to be ripped out and replaced. It went on and on. This would be the quintessential money pit.

How does a professional home inspector handle such a situation? Tell these good people to run away as fast as they could? No, never! Whether they bought the house or not was none of my business. My job was to objectively and unemotionally chronicle everything observed, answer questions and give my clients ballpark repair cost estimates when I felt competent and comfortable doing so.

At the end of the day, an inspector should be satisfied that the information provided regarding the condition of the property will be helpful to the clients during their decision process. They will ultimately decide to run away or go to closing.

Interestingly enough, this couple bought the house, knowing the challenge of restoration which lay ahead. They established a website about their endeavor entitled, "The Pine Level Restoration Project." In it they state "Why in the world did we not run screaming, as recommended by Rudy Platzer, our home inspector?" Did I really say that?

Maybe my report said that between the lines, maybe there was something about my body language, maybe they were reading my mind! It makes no difference, they got the information they needed and they still went forward. The system worked as intended.

**BOTTOM LINE: Factual information is what an inspector should provide; never a personal opinion as to the advisability of purchase.**

# Peeling Paint?

I was asked to look at an old (1890s) wood structure residence in an historic district. The owner told me she was having the wood siding repainted every three to five years because of badly peeling paint. The painter didn't understand why this was happening. He was using high quality paint and following good painting practices. So, why was the paint continually peeling? They were both frustrated.

I asked the client what modifications she had made to the house. She told me she'd had insulation blown into the exterior wall cavities, among other things. I asked her what she had done to the interior surfaces of the walls. She replied that she'd had all the plaster surfaces patched and painted. She was also very proud of the stenciled ceiling borders she had personally painted throughout.

I told her why I thought the paint was peeling. Prior to insulating the walls, the moisture vapor created inside the house from bathing, cooking and even breathing was forced through the plaster and into the exterior wall cavities. And then it was forced

---

The Diary of an Intrepid Home Inspector

through the wood siding on its way outside. After insulation, the inside surface of the siding was cold, whereas before insulating it had been warm. Now the water vapor was condensing on the cold interior siding surface instead of passing through, keeping the wood siding slightly damp. And paint will not adhere to a damp surface.

I went on to explain that this is why a plastic vapor barrier is placed under the drywall in contemporary construction — to keep the water vapor from entering the wall cavities.

She asked what could be done to solve the problem. I told her there was a vapor-barrier latex primer paint that could be applied to the plaster to block the vapor from entering the wall cavities. She replied by asking what would happen to her beautiful stenciled boarders she had spent so many hours painting. "What would become of these?" I shrugged my shoulders sympathetically. They would obviously have to be redone after the vapor barrier primer and finish paint coats were applied. The response was a blank stare.

I watched the house over the years. The exterior was painted again and the paint peeled once again. It was not repainted after that and then the siding become infested with dry rot.

Sometime later the house was heavily damaged by fire and rebuilt. Hopefully the problem was finally solved in the rebuild.

**BOTTOM LINE:  A house is a system.  Modifications of any kind can disrupt the system.  Before any changes are made, possible impacts on the rest of the house should be determined.**


# Band-Aid Fix

I have testified in court cases involving complaints against water-proofers. One of the most popular methods used by these contractors is to install a drainage system around the interior perimeter of a basement to collect water and pump it outside. Sounds like a good idea, doesn't it?

The number one condition by far responsible for basement water entry is deficient grading and drainage around the exterior of the foundation. Usually the condition can be corrected by relatively inexpensive means, e.g. correcting roof gutter slope and cleaning gutters as necessary, extending downspout discharges away from the foundation, maintaining a slope of at least 1" per foot for at least 10 feet around the house, and eliminating "moats" where driveways, walks and landscape borders block drainage. Attending to these elements usually corrects basement flooding.

There are other atypical causes such as ground water flowing under or around the house and broken water lines. But spending ten to twelve thousand dollars to install a fancy collection and pumping system before the less expensive culprits are addressed is, in my opinion, an expensive folly. And, interestingly, most of the houses I have inspected with installed water-proofing systems have one or more of the above described deficiencies around the exterior! It's like using a Band-Aid without addressing the cause of the bleeding.

**BOTTOM LINE:  There may be situations where water-proofing systems might be considered as a last resort, but only after all alternative actions have been addressed.**

# A Trip to the Dark Side

It was late Friday afternoon at the end of a perfect spring day, and the weather forecast for the weekend was more of the same. We were preparing to go to the lake for a couple days of boating when we got a call from one of the national inspection companies for whom I worked over the years as an independent contractor.

There are several of these firms that provide nationwide inspection services to the employee relocation industry. For those of you who may be unfamiliar with the relocation process it goes something like this. When a company decides to relocate an employee, they typically hire a relocation service to handle the move. The relocation process is designed to allow employees to move to their new jobs without the emotional and financial burden of unfinished business at the old location. This includes working with the employee being transferred (they are called "transferees") to help them sell their current house and buy one at the new location. They also arrange for the movement of household goods, all at the expense of the employer. Additionally, if the transferee can't sell the house in a timely manner, the company may buy it and the relocation company will handle this transaction, as well as the eventual sale of the property. Part of the "buy-out" process is a home inspection to determine if there are things in the house which need to be repaired or disclosed. Normally the transferee can make the repairs or deduct the cost of them from the price they are given for the house.

Now, back to the call we received. I had inspected a house for this relocation company the previous fall and the house had remained vacant all winter. Finally there was an offer on the house and the prospective buyers arranged for a pre-purchase home inspection. Their inspector found $7,000 worth of defects which the buyer was asking the relocation company to cover with a reduction in the purchase price.

So much for our week-end plans! I told my client to fax me the buyer's inspection report and that I would return to the property and get back to them. I obtained the current lock box combination from the listing real estate office and we headed to the house, some distance from our office.

At the house, I worked through the list of reported defects. Except for one minor item, which was the result of incomplete winterization of the plumbing system, the report was absolute hog wash! And not surprisingly, the inspector had offered to make the repairs himself for the quoted $7,000!

Was the inspector stupid or dishonest? Legitimate, professional home inspectors never offer repair services because it's a conflict of interest. Was there something going on between the real estate agent and/or the buyer and/or the inspector to whittle the price down? I have no way of knowing.

But I do know one thing — it postponed our weekend plans and I was not a happy camper to be caught up in this inspection scam!

Scams in the real estate/home inspection industry are too common. These two industries should be totally separate. When they become closely related it raises serious conflict of interest questions. Real estate agents and home inspectors who conspire in any way, shape or form should at the very least be disciplined by their respective professional trade organizations. Some of them should possibly even face legal action!

**BOTTOM LINE: Unconscionable activities like this are why I continue to make myself available to provide expert witness testimony against home inspectors who choose to walk on the dark side.**

---

# The Cleanest Kitchen in the World

We were called to inspect a large commercial structure. It was vacant except for an oriental buffet restaurant at one end of the building. As usual, we instructed the real estate agent to notify the tenant when we would be there and approximately how long it would take.

The restaurant dining area was straightforward and uneventful. I then headed for the kitchen. I couldn't believe my eyes when I stepped in!

The kitchen staff was lined up from shortest to tallest, all in spotless white uniforms, some replete with tall chef's hats. They stood at attention with eyes focused straight ahead. As I walked past them I felt like a commanding officer reviewing the troops!

Because the buyer planned to strip out the kitchen appliances and dedicated utility equipment, I concentrated on the basic building components, per se, and the kitchen inspection moved along rather quickly. But I must tell you there has never been a cleaner or tidier kitchen anywhere, ever. Everything from the floor to the last pot and pan sparkled! The kitchen staff remained at attention during my brief visit. It became clear to me that there must have been a miscommunication. My sense is that they were told "an inspector is coming" and they assumed I was from the Health Department.

When I exited through the back door, I turned and said, "Thank you!" I got a resounding "thank you" response along with a unanimous bow and grin. They must have thought their kitchen had passed the inspection with flying colors!

**BOTTOM LINE: Just another interesting experience in the life of an intrepid home inspector.**


# Pre-approved

It was a new house, nearly finished. My client was relocating from another state and was anxious for completion and closing. As we moved through the house, I noticed a plumber working under a bar cabinet in the family room. He was hooking up a sink, a simple enough task. About an hour and a half later, we happened by again. This time the plumber gave me a wry smile and said, "Hey Mr. Inspector, you wanna inspect this sink?" At that he pulled a code inspection tag out of his shirt pocket and said, "Well, knock yourself out inspecting the plumbing in this house 'cause it's already been approved."

Lessons learned:
1. The plumber was definitely milking the job.
2. The code inspector approved the job before it was completed.
3. Besides exposing his crack, the plumber also gave us some interesting insights into how "the system" works!

**BOTTOM LINE: Invariably the cost of wasteful work practices is passed along to the buyer in the cost of the house. As for reliance on code inspections…hummm; need I say more?**

# The Million Dollar Baby

My client was relocating into my market area to become the CEO of a large corporation. He called to schedule a whole-house inspection just two days prior to closing. He told me that the custom home had been built under contract but the owner had walked prior to its completion. It was the only home available in the neighborhood his wife had selected and so he had signed a contract to buy it.

He relayed that he had wanted the house inspected from the outset but the real estate agent had talked him out of it. "Why would you waste money having this lovely new home, built by a top builder in the area, inspected?" she had chided him. At the ninth hour he thought better of it and wanted to know if I could inspect it on such short notice. I was able to rearrange my schedule and visited the house the next day.

The house was a very large, two-story wood frame structure built on a poured concrete foundation. The finished basement had a glass walled walk-out at the rear. The site was level from the street up to the front of the house, after which it sloped rather dramatically into a deep ravine at the rear. This made the lower-level walk-out family room possible. It was a beautiful setting!

To execute this type of house plan, a "cut and fill" excavation was required. In other words, soil was removed from under the front of the house and pulled back into the ravine to provide support for the rear of the house. This is a common practice on such a site, but it has to be executed properly to preclude settlement problems.

Understanding this, the first thing I did upon arriving was to walk down the slope along both sides of the house to view the foundation. To my dismay, I found large vertical cracks on both sides. They were typical settlement cracks — narrow at the bottom and wide at the top. The rear of the house was settling into the fill portion of the excavation.

What would cause this? First, if the soil was not mechanically compacted as it was being placed, the weight of the foundation and the house would quickly compact it, causing settlement to occur. An alternative, which was obviously not followed, would have involved placing supports such as pilings or piers through the fill and down to the original, naturally compacted soil to support the foundation. This would have been a desirable option in this case since it was a very large and heavy house.

Now, however, there was a problem — a very big problem! I entered the house and went directly to the lower level. Once in the family room and performed a very scientific test. I took a golf ball from my inspection case and placed it on the carpet. It immediately and quickly rolled toward the rear wall. I would use a level later to document the exact amount of settlement. I then walked through the rest of the house. There were tell-tale signs of settlement throughout.

Every house settles to some extent over time — most of it can be tolerated and easily dealt with. But differential settlement such as this would require dramatic corrective action. And, it was highly possible that the settlement would continue for some time into the future. My report would so reflect.

Because closing was so near at hand, I called my client immediately with the bad news. He was incredulous and said he would immediately call the builder. The builder, in turn, called his attorney and a message from the attorney was on my answering machine by the time I returned to my office. It went something like, "We'll see you in court…!" It was quite a rant. I returned his call and told him that the builder would be wise to spend his money fixing the problem instead of running his attorney's meter. I was not the cause of this problem; the builder was. My report would not change! And I went on to inform him that I was in the habit of writing "bullet-proof" reports. I ended our call with the assertion that I would look forward to facing him in court if that's what lay ahead.

Fast-forward — the closing was rescheduled. At my recommendation a geotechnical engineering firm made core borings at the site to produce stratified soil samples for analysis. They determined not only had the soil not been compacted, but the fill also contained tree stumps! It was difficult for me to believe; this was a multi-million dollar house!

I also recommended that a licensed structural engineer be engaged to recommend corrective actions. My client accepted the builder's offer to pay for an engineer which, in my opinion, was a big mistake. (As in, "He who pays the piper calls the tune!") The engineer, who was not licensed, recommended repairs which I considered superficial. And he failed to address the future settlement problems which were axiomatic! The builder made only the minor repairs suggested by the engineer and my client went to closing. I had won the battle and lost the war! My client had succumbed to the opinion of his builder's engineer — no matter how inept or corrupt. It was beyond my control.

Incidentally, the house had many other flaws, some serious. And it is also quite interesting that this "top builder" went bankrupt within a year. I subsequently inspected other houses built by him in this very upscale neighborhood, and all had major problems. Contrary to the real estate agent's endorsement, this was definitely a bad builder!

**BOTTOM LINE: Be careful out there. It doesn't matter who built your new home. It still needs to be inspected by a qualified independent home inspector who has no axe to grind.**

# The Farm with 100 Barns

Well, it didn't have 100, but it sure as hell seemed like it! Actually, there were 10 outbuildings, including an abandoned, luxury three-hole outhouse!

It was an old, vacant farmhouse with a lot of problems. It was three counties away, which I considered out of my usual market area, but I accepted the job since it was for a repeat client.

It was a cold, cold winter day with a howling wind and several inches of snow on the ground. There was only enough heat in the house to keep the pipes from freezing. It was one of those days when I went back to my truck from time to time just to get warm. It was one of those days when I had to use a lead pencil because it was too cold for my ballpoint. One of those days when I wished it was summer. One of those days when I wondered why the hell I was in this business anyway!

Now, about the ten outbuildings; the client wanted them all inspected. They were in terrible condition. I was tempted to just say, "Tear them all down!" But that would not have been helpful to the buyer. He would want to know enough specifics to judge for himself whether repairs were practicable or whether, in fact, they should be demolished. I called the client and told him that if I were to inspect these structures it would be on an hourly rate in addition to the fee quoted for the house. He said, "Do it." It took two days, including travel time, to finish the job. Ruth felt sorry for me and came along to help on the second day. The report went on and on, listing the many structural, roofing and electrical problems found. I even commented on the outhouse; for all I knew he wanted to keep it as an historical treasure!

**BOTTOM LINE: We were called and responded, the client was happy, and we got paid. It was just another couple of (very cold) days in the life of an intrepid home inspector.**

# Who Do You Believe?

I use an electronic "sniffer" to locate gas leaks at pipe joints and unions, gas meters, gas-fired appliances, pool heaters and occasionally underground gas service lines. I can usually smell a gas leak, but the instrument helps me locate it. And, it is more authoritative to say "using an electronic gas detection meter I located a gas leak at the water heater shut-off valve."

I had just identified such a leak at a house and notified the seller. (Normally, we do not discuss findings with anyone before presenting our report to our client, but we break that rule when safety is concerned.) She was grateful for the information and said she would call her plumber right away.

The next morning I got a call from her saying her plumber was on-site and could not find the leak. She sounded agitated. I told her that I was just leaving for an appointment near her house and would stop by her place on my way.

When I arrived the plumber was still there. I used my sniffer to pinpoint the leak. He said, "I soaped that valve and there ain't no leak!" (Some plumbers use a soap solution which can bubble when brushed over a leak.) The woman glared at me.

I asked her if she would mind smelling in the vicinity of the gas valve. Reluctantly, she agreed. I asked her if she smelled anything. She responded that she detected an unpleasant odor. I told her that was an agent introduced by the gas supplier to make leaks noticeable. I left, leaving the rest to her, but cautioned her that the gas leak really needed to be corrected and would be so noted in my report.

**BOTTOM LINE: Who did she believe? If you were the seller of this house who would you believe?**


# Something Fishy

The house was built in 1912 by a renowned engineer of the day. It was an enormous estate. The mansion was a huge, three-story, cut limestone structure. The carriage house alone had 3,000 square feet of quite accommodating servants' quarters on the upper two floors. There was an Olympic-sized pool as well as tennis and basketball courts. The carriage house was located at some distance from the mansion and was connected by an underground tunnel. There was so much to look at! It took me two ten-hour days to inspect the place. The fee we quoted was commensurate with the amount of time we knew it would take.

Now let me digress for a moment. We were called by the buyer to inspect this property and we scheduled it. Then, we got a call from the listing agent to cancel the inspection. (He just happened to have me on his "shit list" and I knew it!) I called him. He told me that the buyer had decided to use another inspector. Really! He was the listing agent, not the agent the buyer was using. I smelled something fishy! I called the buyer and he told me the listing agent had informed him that the sellers would rather have someone else inspect their house.

As luck would have it, I knew the listing agent's broker quite well; in fact, I went through business school with him. I drove to his office. I told him the story and informed him that if his agent was successful in keeping me from inspecting that house, I would definitely file a lawsuit — we'd let the judge decide if this was a case of restraining trade.

He knew me and he knew I was serious. I felt that I had to "plant my flag" in this instance to establish a precedent! The broker stepped in, and I inspected the property as planned.

Now back to the inspection. It was a fantastic house, way ahead of its time in terms of the mechanical equipment, plumbing, and heating systems. It was built like a fortress; in a word it was "overbuilt" by today's residential standards.

Did I find things to comment on? Yes, of course. This was a 1912 structure. It had a couple of flat roof sections, in addition to the original slate roof, all of which needed some repair. There was absolutely no insulation in the house, making it an energy money pit. There were a few plumbing issues. But the electrical system, while complex and time consuming to inspect, was in great shape. The home had been maintained professionally and had many upgrades over the years. It was a real treasure and my report reflected that. It was a joy to inspect.

I can't resist pointing to one of the many unique features of this house. The rather small foyer opened into a huge two-story great room. The lower walls were walnut paneled, while the second-story portions were covered in beautiful alfresco oil paintings. The coffered ceiling was also covered in similar paintings framed by walnut beams. And, opposite the front entry there was a second story balcony featuring the pipes of a concert organ, which I was told was still functional. Certainly not your everyday house!

**BOTTOM LINE: The listing agent no doubt eventually received a copy of my report. Did he think he intimidated me into giving it high marks? Frankly, who cares? I produced an objective report, as I always do. I won't tell you what I still think of that agent! I did my job, my client and the sellers were happy and that's all that matters.**


# Cottage on the Water

Who wouldn't be taken by this location? A small, cute, inviting house, only feet from the river. But, my long-standing knowledge of this area raised a question about this location.

I asked my client, "Did the real estate agent tell you anything about this location?" "No, why?" she replied. "Because," I explained, "This house is in a flood plain." "Oh my, what does that mean?" she replied. I explained to her that in the case of an abnormally wet spring that put the river over its banks this house could be at least partially underwater.

"Oh no!" she exclaimed. This was followed by a long, pensive silence and then she retreated to the back porch step where she proceeded to cry uncontrollably. I had just burst her bubble.

After regaining her composure, she explained that she had planned to live in the cottage until she could replace it with her dream home. She was still having trouble coming to grips with the scenario I had related. I reassured her that the surveyor, and/or the appraiser, and/or the mortgage lender would confirm what I had told her.

I asked her if she wanted me to complete the inspection and she said she did. I found evidence of past flooding once inside. I completed the inspection, gave her the report, got my check, wished her well and left. I have no idea whether she bought the place or not. I made the most professional disclosure of which I was capable and left wondering about the outcome.

**BOTTOM LINE: You can lead your client to the water but she may want to live there anyway!**

# Get All the Information

I was inspecting a beautiful waterfront property with two floors of luxurious living space built over a large boathouse. It was very good construction throughout with many custom features and a knockout water view. This was every boater's dream home!

There was no boat in the boathouse which made inspecting it easier. But, this house was occupied and it occurred to me that a boathouse without a boat is like a kiss without a squeeze. So, I asked the real estate agent how deep the water was in the boathouse. She replied "about six feet." That would be enough to accommodate a boat of the size intended for this space, I thought. "How about the water depth in the channel behind the boathouse," I asked. "I don't know," she abruptly replied. She then excused herself and disappeared. I was curious because without proper channel depth the boathouse would not be useable and the property value would be greatly diminished.

As it turned out, everybody in the area (except the real estate agent) knew that the channel was no longer navigable! There was not enough water to get a boat into or out of the boathouse unless an enormously expensive dredging project was undertaken! I'm not saying the agent knew or should have known. I am saying you may not get all the information you need from a salesperson. "Buyer Beware!" is always the best guideline. Be sure you get all the information needed to make a good buying decision, whether from your home inspector, local residents or any other available source. There may be one omitted piece of information that could make all the difference.

**BOTTOM LINE: Real estate people may or may not know important facts about a property. But it really makes no difference; it's the buyer's responsibility to get all the information needed to make an informed buying decision. And, one more time — get the information on the condition of the house from a professional home inspector, not a real estate agent.**

# Beautiful Upscale House

It was a four-year old, upscale custom home in a beautiful setting; the kind of house that's a pleasure to work through.

It was a joy indeed, and I was finding only a few minor tweaks. The crawl space was my last stop, but I expected it to be a nice one compared to many of the nasty ones I had crawled.

Surprise! There was no vapor barrier over the dirt floor and the ventilation was inadequate. All the wood framing elements were covered by mildew. The damp environment was a set-up for microbiological attack. And if mildew liked it, could a dry rot attack be far behind? I recommended evaluation by an environmental specialist and also recommended increased ventilation and the addition of a vapor barrier.

And now, for the rest of the story: It was a nice house with some problems in the crawl space that needed to be addressed. The good news was that there was no damage to the wood framing members at the time of the inspection. Fix the problems, buy the house and live happily ever after. This could have easily turned out to be a win-win scenario.

Au contraire! The sellers became quite defensive. They said the builder had a fine reputation and could not possibly be responsible for such deficiencies! They would call him to debunk my report.

---

My clients called me to pass along the builder's reaction. He said he had never heard of such things and that obviously, "I didn't know what the hell I was talking about!" I told them I had committed my opinion to writing and would be glad to review a written response from him. Maybe I could learn something! The sellers agreed with the builder; after all, this company had been building houses for forty years.

I did some detective work. I found that the father who had founded the construction company had recently retired. His son, who had an MBA from a well-known east coast university, now ran the business.

I asked myself, "What did this kid learn in business school? Has he ever held a hammer in his hand? Is he stupid or just a poor businessman, or both? Whatever!"

The deal did not go through; a big "no win" for everyone. Damn! I always felt bad when something like this happened, but it was a human nature sort of thing — and that's outside my sphere of expertise!

**BOTTOM LINE: Too often I have inspected houses constructed by builders with "good reputations", only to find glaring inadequacies. Any builder can make a mistake for any number of reasons. Buying from a reputable builder is a good start, but every house bears critiquing by a professional inspector. The best builders view an inspection as a learning experience. They fix problems that are found and become even better, protecting and enhancing their reputations as a result. The others, in my experience, are headed for civil or bankruptcy court.**

# A Trip Down Memory Lane

In the 1940's, the National Cash Register Company (NCR) headquartered in Dayton, had a community outreach program for kids. (This was before the era of TV, computer games and cell phones.) They had a large auditorium at their plant site and every Saturday morning they put on a stage show followed by a full-length kid's movie like "The Little Rascals" — along with Popeye and Bugs Bunny cartoons.

The emcee at these events was a young entertainer who was a local household name. We kids loved him! But then, I'm reminded that this book is about home inspecting.

The house I was to inspect was in an estate, the owner having died quite unexpectedly. As I did my initial walkthrough it appeared as though someone was still living there, although I knew better. There were still clothes in the closets, and pictures and memorabilia everywhere. And then it dawned on me. The deceased owner was the man who had entertained me at NCR on Saturday mornings! Suddenly this became a personal experience; I got a lump in my throat!

While my professional focus was on the work before me, I couldn't escape the many pictures of his family, as well as those taken with famous people of the day. And, the numerous awards and trophies garnered throughout his professional life. He had become a successful businessman and community leader and was actively involved in a number of charities. It was as though I was walking through his lifetime successes in his footsteps! A powerful experience, indeed!

I don't recall much about the house, but I do have a vivid picture of the man out of my past, who entertained me on Saturday mornings so many years before.

**BOTTOM LINE: It's generally not good form to become emotionally involved when inspecting a house but in this case I found it impossible to avoid.**

# Why Would Anyone Buy This House?

The house was on acreage just south of a development of high-end homes. It was a small, older structure just off the road at the foot of a hill.

I arrived early, which gave me a chance to scope out the lay of the land. I couldn't believe my eyes as I approached the house! There was a huge negative slope in the soil around all four sides of the foundation. I just knew this concrete block foundation would be a problem.

My client still had not arrived. I introduced myself to the occupants and got their permission to enter the basement. It was worse than I imagined; all four concrete block walls were pushed in and near collapse. Why would my client give this house a second look?

As I was leaving the house to wait for my client, he drove up. I expressed my concern about the foundation and wouldn't have been surprised had he terminated the inspection at that point. Instead, he told me he was aware of the problem, and went on to tell me his plan for building his dream home on the top of the hill. The existing house would be a temporary shelter, to be torn down once the new house was complete.

He had two questions for me:

1. Was the house habitable in the near term?

2. What could be done, on a temporary basis, to preclude the foundation collapse?

I told him my whole house inspection would answer his first question. I went on to tell him what I would do to resolve the foundation problem. First, I would move the electric water heater from the basement to a closet on the main floor. It was the only mechanical equipment in the basement as the house was heated with electric baseboard heaters. Then I would have gravel trucked in from a nearby quarry, filling the basement with gravel through the basement windows on all four sides. This would create an equal pressure on the inside of the walls and stabilize the foundation. He was ecstatic!

The rest of the house passed muster with only a couple of minor items. My client was pleased and my curiosity was quelled.

**BOTTOM LINE: An inspector should not second-guess his or her client's intentions. There's no way to know what's going through their minds. And, buyers would do well to tell their inspector, up front, about any plans they may have for the property so he or she can be ready to offer helpful insights.**

# The Big Bang Theory

I had inspected the house in the middle of the winter. It had a central forced-air furnace with central air conditioning. The furnace checked out fine, but I didn't run the air conditioner because operating it in cold weather could damage the equipment.

The next spring, my client called regarding a problem with the air conditioner.

---

It seems they heard a loud "bang" when they turned it on for the first time and then the system shut down. I went to the house to take a first-hand look.

A one-year "home warranty" was included with the purchase of this house, so the first thing my clients did was call the "warranty" company.

The company sent out a local heating and air conditioning contractor to take care of the problem. The technician who responded told them that the furnace/air conditioner was installed improperly and as a result it had a major malfunction. Since the improper installation was a pre-existing condition, the "warranty" would not cover it. But, the repair contractor could fix the installation problems for $700 and then the "warranty" company would pay for the damage to the unit — estimated at about $1000. Thus, he would save them around $300. And, of course, the $700 part of the deal was offered only because they were such nice people and he felt sorry for them and wanted to give them a break.

Well, guess who my clients were looking at to pay the $700 to correct the pre-existing problem which I should have found during my inspection? You guessed it – me!

I looked the equipment over and told my clients that it was installed in accordance with the manufacturers' installation instructions and the local code. I also found the condition causing the "bang" and the subsequent shut down. Typically, the fan in this unit was used to circulate warm air in the winter and cold air in the summer. The fan operated at a faster speed when the air conditioner was switched on because cold air is heavier than warm air and needs an extra push to get to second story bedrooms.

I reminded them that I had not switched the air conditioner on during my mid-winter inspection because it is not wise to do so. When they started the air conditioner, the faster fan speed pushed a higher volume of air through the air distribution ductwork and a weak piece of the duct on the return-air side collapsed and blocked the air flow, causing the unit to shut down. If a minor repair was made to the ductwork and the equipment reset, I felt quite sure the problem would be resolved. The cost would probably be between $125 and $150 and would be covered by the "warranty." The $700 and $1000 repair work? An obvious scam! I gave them a letter to that effect.

My clients called the repair contractor and told him they would give him another chance to look at the situation in light of my evaluation. The contractor returned, apologized for the mistake and made the repairs according to my suggestions. The unit performed well, the "warranty" company paid the bill, and my clients paid only the normal co-pay spelled out in the "warranty" contract.

Now, why do I continually use quotation marks when I use the word "warranty?" The home "warranty" programs with which I am familiar are not really warranties in the strict sense of the word. They are service contracts. This means that the service contractor will keep equipment in properly functioning condition for a specified period of time (usually one year) for flat fee co-pay. Typically, faulty equipment does not have to be replaced and parts used for repairs need not be new. All of this can be found in the small print and may vary from company to company.

Home "warranty" companies are glad to sign onto these contracts even though they have no clue as to the age or condition of the equipment covered. Experience tells them that, statistically, the odds of failure are on their side.

**BOTTOM LINE: People often ask me whether I recommend buying these service contracts. I tell them to read the entire contract. If the equipment covered by the contract is very old, I think there may be some value. By all means, I encourage them to understand what the contract will and will not cover to enable them to make an informed decision. If the contract is paid for by the seller, the buyer should still be aware of what coverage will be afforded to avoid unrealistic expectations.**

# Things Aren't Always As They Seem

It was a 40-something years old house. I had inspected all elements except the attic. I got my ladder out of the truck and headed upstairs toward the access hatch. The seller had kept an eye on me throughout the entire inspection; nothing wrong with that.

"Where are you headed?" she asked. "Into the attic," I replied. Her body language told me she hadn't expected me to inspect the attic. What would I find up there?

As soon as I popped up through the hatch I saw the evidence of a previous fire. The white shellac on the structural roof members was the tell-tale sign. When fire restoration contractors finish replacing badly damaged framing members they spray the less damaged, charred members and most of the rest of the attic framework and roof deck to knock down the fire smell. This attic was a typical fire restoration.

I yelled down to my clients, "There has been a fire up here." "What? We weren't told about any fire!" was the response. Then there was a rather long pause of silence. "Yes, we did recently have a fire," stated the seller. Obviously it hadn't been disclosed to the buyers.

After carefully evaluating the structure, I told my clients that the repair work appeared to be satisfactory and shouldn't be a problem for them. This seemed to settle them down.

I was interested to know the cause of the fire so I asked the seller if an investigation had been conducted by the fire officials. She replied that it was determined to be an electrical problem in the wall beside the fireplace chimney. This seemed plausible judging from the location of the repair work; most of the structural members around the chimney in the attic had been replaced. But there was another nagging piece of the puzzle that I could not put out of my mind.

Earlier I had inspected the fireplace and flue and told my clients that the chimney was a dangerous fire hazard. There were large cracks throughout the full length of the terra-cotta flue liner. The cracks were old and in retrospect my sense was that they were there when this fire occurred. I asked the seller if they had used the fireplace since the fire. She said, "No, the fire occurred in the spring"; we were now into late summer. So, it made sense that this fire hazard existed at the time of the fire, yet was not determined to be the cause of the fire. Hmmmmmm.

In any case, I had called my client's attention to the flue lining problem and recommended they have it I replaced by a certified chimney sweep or reputable mason.

**BOTTOM LINE: An ember can find its way through a crack in a flue liner, attach itself to a nearby structural member with an already lowered combustion temperature and start a fire. Any crack in a clay flue liner is potentially dangerous and should be identified and addressed before using a fireplace!**


# A Lesson in Reporting

It was an old, Spanish-style structure with a flat roof. The once fashionable neighborhood had lost its luster and many of the homes were in a state of disrepair. Why would anyone be interested? I've asked myself that question many times, but I would never ask a client. It's none of my business.

As we worked our way through this very large house, we were met at every turn by water-stained ceilings and walls. It was quite obvious that the flat roof had been leaking for a very long time. The evidence was everywhere!

But not to worry! The clients informed me that the listing featured a new roof! And, they were informed by the sellers that the roofers had just completed it days before the inspection. My clients were excited about that. They loved the house and the roof had been their greatest concern.

We were nearing the end of the inspection, and it was time to mount the roof. I extended my ladder, went up and over the parapet and was introduced to the new roof. The covering was asphalt roll roofing, the least expensive material for a flat roof. It definitely would not have been my choice for this application. Moreover, the workmanship was amateurish. Just about everything that could be wrong with a flat roof installation was staring me in the face; what a mess! I was disappointed for my clients and pondered how they would react to the bad news.

My job now was to carefully critique this roof and document the many things wrong with it. Then I would recommend a second opinion from a reputable flat roofing specialist. My sense was that a competent roofer would recommend removal and replacement. I descended to relate my findings to my clients, the sellers and their man-and-wife listing agents. The agents were immediately outraged! How could I possibly be saying such things about a brand new roof? I responded by saying that my report was an objective portrayal of what I had observed. I added that I was so confident about the deficiencies I had observed that I would even be comfortable defending my report in a court of law.

Little did I know! About a year later, I was subpoenaed to appear in a court case regarding this roof. The plaintiff buyers alleged that the roof started leaking throughout the house soon after they took occupancy, causing tens of thousands of dollars' worth of damages. They claimed they had been told by the agents that I was not a roofer and therefore not qualified to pass judgment on the roof. They convinced the plaintiffs to complete the deal.

I was called to testify by the listing real estate company's defense attorney. She asked me about my education, professional credentials and affiliations as well as my experience. She was able to get into the record that everyone in the real estate community knew how thorough and competent I was. Wow! What an endorsement! All the praise an inspector would ever want to hear, especially coming from the real estate folks!

She then produced my inspection report, which she had also subpoenaed. She carefully walked me through the portion of the report dealing with the roof and asked me to explain everything in detail. Her argument, obviously, was that the plaintiff's had been given competent advice, in writing, by an expert, which they chose to ignore. And now, they were blaming others for their own irresponsibility! She won the case for the defendants.

I felt bad for my clients especially since my testimony was used to their detriment. Subsequent to the trial, I called them to explain that I had no choice but to tell the truth. They understood. While they were disappointed in the outcome, they didn't blame me.

**BOTTOM LINE: Report writing is an essential element in the art of home inspection. You never know what path any given report might follow. It should always be totally objective, well-written and technically "bullet proof."**

# Problems Swept Under the Rugs

There were throw rugs everywhere in this upscale, well-decorated house. I don't normally concern myself with the cosmetics of a house but the sheer number of rugs caught my attention. They were everywhere, on the hardwood, the tile and even over carpets. Out of curiosity, I lifted one and then another. Under each one was a surprise waiting to be discovered! Torn carpeting, broken tiles and stained hardwood. I thought this was worthy of disclosing to my clients and so I did. They needed to know that they would face numerous repair or replacements of floor coverings unless the throw rugs were included in the final sales contract!

**BOTTOM LINE: You never know what problems could be simply swept under the rugs.**

# What Should an Inspection Report Look Like?

The house was vacant. There was a conspicuous sign on the kitchen counter which read "Inspection Report." In front of it was a small piece of paper, which at first glance appeared to be a guest check from a cheap restaurant. It was rubber stamped at the top with the name of a home inspector. Hand-written on the face were the words, "Everything checked out OK."

WOW! Who would call this an inspection report? Anyone who would proudly display this piece of paper and refer to it as an inspection report should be ashamed of themselves for exposing their ignorance! Anyone who actually paid for this almost humorous misrepresentation of a home inspection got ripped off big time! Or, perhaps it was exactly the kind of report the seller or their agent wanted? I explained to my client that despite this report, it was highly improbable that "everything would check out OK." And, that at the end of my three-hour inspection, they would receive my 42-page inspection report which would document everything I found. My clients saw through this sham and we proceeded to inspect the house. It turned out to be a good house, but as predicted, "Everything" was not "OK".

**BOTTOM LINE: A professional inspection report will document the inspector's observations and findings on every major system of the house. It should include information on the age and condition of components and address their life expectancies. The terms "everything" and "OK" are usually not in the vocabulary of a professional home inspector!**

# What Can Happen to a House when People Move Out?

When my client took possession of the house after closing they found the vinyl flooring in the kitchen was gouged and torn. He called the sellers to complain only to be told that it was that way when they bought the house. "Your inspector should have found that," he was told. And so he called me. I reminded my client of the time we spent in that kitchen checking the appliances, receptacles, light fixtures, windows, walls, ceilings and floors. He agreed that we had been in there long enough to have seen such horrendous damage to the floor. I asked him where the damage was and he said it was in front of the large refrigerator, which the sellers had taken with them. It became obvious to both of us that whoever moved that refrigerator out of the kitchen had not properly protected the floors. At his request, I wrote him a letter stating such.

**BOTTOM LINE: The home inspection profession definitely gave me many lessons in human nature. I like to call it "The Good, the Bad and the Ugly 101." We recommended, in writing in our report, that our clients conduct a pre-closing walk-through to identify these kinds of things and preclude these types of problems.**

# Another Type of Winter "Flue"

I was called by an attorney to investigate an alleged faulty roof installation. I went to the claimant's house and conducted the roof inspection. The owner of the house was a registered nurse with two pre-school age children in the house. She engaged me in conversation and told me how dissatisfied she was with the contractor who installed the roof. Then she mentioned that he had also installed a new furnace to replace the older one which the contractor had called "unsafe." She stated she never hesitated to authorize the furnace replacement because of the health concerns for her daughters. I asked if I could take a look at the furnace to be sure it had been installed properly. She consented and thanked me for my concern.

It was a very cold winter day and the furnace had been operating the entire time I was in the house. I entered the utility room and took my electronic gas detector from my inspection kit (this tool detects both raw and exhaust gases). As soon as I turned the meter on, I was given a dangerous reading! I first checked for raw gas leaks at all of the gas supply connections and valves but found no leakage there. Then I checked the flue pipe draft diverter. This is a device on top of the furnace to allow air to enter and provide a draft to push exhaust gas up through the flue and to the outside above the roof. Although the furnace had been replaced, the flue pipe had not. My assessment was that the flue was defective when connected to the old furnace and then reconnected to the new furnace without examination or repair.

Upon further inspection, I determined that the flue was blocked by debris, it was too close to combustible wood framing members in the attic and it lacked mechanical joint fasteners. I explained the situation to the nurse/owner and recommended that she and her children leave the house until the unsafe conditions could be corrected. Needless to say, she was extremely concerned that her children had been exposed to the exhaust gases which most assuredly contained some level of carbon monoxide! And, by the way, the furnace was installed in a closet that did not have proper fresh air supply and lacked the required clearance to the combustible closet door!

When I reported my findings to the client's attorney, he was most appreciative of my helping our client avoid a potentially dangerous situation. He also commented that he was "really anxious to meet this contractor in court." I testified on both the poor roof and furnace installations and we won. In addition to receiving prompt payment of my fee, the "thank you" phone call I received from the nurse made my day!

**BOTTOM LINE: If a contractor did one thing wrong, he may well have done other things wrong. My policy is to look beyond the issue(s) at hand. If other anomalies are found, they are reported to the attorney. I've found that a one-issue case can sometime become a multi-issue case with a better chance of winning.**

# Houses Completed On Time

Plat homes, often called "production houses" or "cookie cutter houses," are far more likely to be completed on time than custom built homes. This is because the plat development is viewed as the project and the individual houses are parts of a very carefully orchestrated plan.

The entire process moves forward in a way which manages the total resources of labor, material and machines in the most efficient manner. Certainly there are glitches such as bad weather and material shortages which can temporarily slow the process, however most often these homes are ready for occupancy on or very close to the target date.

I often hear complaints from people building custom homes that it's taking longer than expected. Sometimes a lot longer! Why?

By definition, these homes are one-of-a-kind and have never been built before. (I capriciously refer to these houses as "Research and Development" projects.) This makes precise planning difficult. The construction "bugs" that invariably crop up haven't been worked through like they are early on in a repetitive production process. The trades-people have to work through many custom details as they piece the project together. The electrical, plumbing, heating and air conditioning, carpentry, flooring and even painting contractors have a much harder scheduling job because of all the unknowns and delays typically encountered. As a result, custom homes are rarely completed on time.

One notable exception is "Home-a-Rama" type houses. They are always completed on time — sometimes just hours before "Showtime!" These are highly customized homes built on a tight production schedule. And if mistakes are made there may not be enough time to correct them properly.

People often buy these houses for the thrill and prestige of living in a Home-a-Rama show house and the decorator touches that are included in the price. I have been called a number of times by attorneys whose clients have moved in with high expectations only to find a host of problems, likely due to the last minute crunch of meeting the deadline.

If you are building a custom home be sure to choose a general contractor with a proven track record in building homes of the type and size you want. I've been involved as an expert witness in far too many cases where a general contractor came up short and wound up being sued due to his incompetence. With custom homes there is a greater propensity for mistakes, even big mistakes.

In my opinion, custom homes should always be inspected during construction. Very large, expensive structures are likely to be followed by an architect — usually the designer. He or she will visit the building site often as the construction progresses to provide technical supervision and oversight. This is a good approach, but can be quite expensive. Consequently, it is seldom used except for the most costly projects. An alternate approach is to have a series of "progress inspections" done by a professional home inspector. I have done a number of these over the years and never cease to be amazed at what I find.

I've seen problems with foundations, framing, electrical, plumbing, heating, air conditioning, ventilation, insulation, wall cladding, grading and drainage, etc. In fact, I've seen virtually everything that can go wrong with any house go wrong during custom home construction.

**BOTTOM LINE: I've had many more builders thank me for my help than those considering me just a royal pain in the posterior. Either way, the owner who is paying for my services is the benefactor — sometimes in a very big way!**

# The Very Vacant House

A lawyer asked me to look at a newly constructed house. He explained that the owner had refused to close on it, due to a number of major defects. He wanted me to confirm the number and severity of these issues. The builder was accusing the buyer of being "melodramatic."

I met the would-be owner, a young engineer, at the property. The house was built on acreage which he had purchased some years previous to the construction. This was the site he and his wife chose to build their dream home — the one where they would raise their family.

It was a two-story, wood framed structure built on a concrete block foundation with full basement.

As we walked through the house, it was immediately clear to me that the problems the young engineer had identified were not being exaggerated. Floors were grossly out of level; the rear of the foundation had collapsed during construction and had not been properly repaired. There were many other major issues. I couldn't believe my eyes!

I still find it difficult to believe the number and severity of the problems I confirmed. This may well have been the worst new construction I had ever seen.

I asked the engineer about the builder. He said that he had been at a home show where a national home builder had been an exhibitor. He looked over their glossy, full-color marketing material and listened intently to their hard sell on the history and capability of the company. He was sold.

As the house went up, he called the site superintendent's attention to the many mistakes that he saw being made. For the most part, his pleadings were ignored and the construction continued.

The house was completed and the bank wanted to close on the loan. The builder refused to address the problems and the bank persisted. If he closed, the mortgage would not only be on the house, but would include the acreage which he owned outright. He felt trapped.

Moreover, he had school-aged children and his wife, a school teacher, wanted to get them enrolled in the local school system. The school year was soon to begin. His dilemma became even bigger.

I wrote a scathing report on this house. The engineer and his attorney were both grateful. I heard no more from either of them. This happens frequently and I presume it is because my report was helpful in reaching a resolution.

Now, for the rest of the story: This property was just a short distance off a major highway which I often used. Every now and then, when time permitted, I would drive by this house to see what was going on. It remained vacant during the first school year, and the second, and the third. Tall weeds covered a once well-maintained lawn and even covered the gravel lane. The dream house had become deserted!

After a few years, I stopped driving by. I could only imagine what kind of a mess this turned out to be. Obviously a long and nasty legal fight — and quite possibly accompanied by domestic strife.

**BOTTOM LINE: Building a dream home can become a nightmare. It happens to good people all too often! What a shame! Construction progress inspections by a professional home inspector might have averted this situation!**

# What is an Expert Witness?

Most of us have seen "expert witnesses" testify in televised, high profile court cases. But, until I became one I knew little about this daunting role.

The need for expert witnesses arises in legal cases where technical issues are involved. Lawyers and judges know the law but need help to understand the technical details involved in these cases. And, the lay people serving as jurors also need subject matter specialists to help them understand technical details. Enter the expert witness.

In my practice, I provide information on construction defects on both residential and commercial structures. I typically testify regarding unacceptable building practices and a myriad of other issues affecting safety and habitability. I offer my opinions on the nature of the defects, how they might have been avoided and corrective actions needed.

It is very important to underscore the word "opinion." An expert is the only witness granted the right to offer an opinion on what has happened and why. All other witnesses are limited to testifying only about what they saw, heard or know to be factual. This puts a heavy burden on the expert. While being allowed to offer opinions, those opinions must nonetheless be supported by solid research, and/or personal experience, education or background.

Nowadays there are usually one or more experts testifying on each side of a complex dispute. Every expert's qualifications are reviewed beforehand by the judge, who determines if they are qualified to offer opinions in the specifics of the case before the court. Isn't it interesting that these experts, in the process of instructing the court, become part of the adversarial process when offering different opinions! One might testify that the technical aspects of the case are "Black" and the other that they are "White."

I'm often asked how it can be that experts, who are testifying under oath, can give conflicting testimony. Quite simply, there are different views on just about everything! Professional views are no different. And the more technically involved issues are, the more contentious they may become. And it is these complex cases that tend to go to trial because the litigants could not arrive at a common, acceptable understanding of the circumstances or causes leading to the dispute.

Interestingly, one of the first questions typically asked of an expert by the opposing attorney is, "Are you being paid for the testimony you are giving today?" The answer is always. "Yes." Experts are paid for their time while testifying, as well as their time examining evidence, reading pertinent documents, doing relevant research, advising attorneys and preparing for their court appearance. This question concerning compensation is intended to portray the expert as a "hired gun". Casting doubt among the jurors on the credibility and objectivity of the expert is an often used tactic. The expert must therefore not only be technically competent but must also take every opportunity to assure the jury he or she is totally neutral and reliable.

An expert's testimony can often be the turning point in a case. An expert who has done his or her homework by carefully and thoroughly researching technical issues, case documentation, and evidence collected at the site will be prepared for every technical question posed. But that is just the beginning. He or she must also be able to present a cogent and compelling explanation of the technical issues that all the participants can understand. And the expert must be ready to defend his or her opinions without becoming contentious even under the most aggressive of cross examinations.

**BOTTOM LINE: It is important work, difficult work, satisfying work, fun work! I have a number of interesting (and even a few humorous) courtroom stories which I've shared in other parts of this book.**

# Home Inspectors Are Not Perfect

Any competent home inspector will tell you he or she does not have X-ray vision or a crystal ball. Home inspections are visual in nature and some problems can elude visual observation. That's not a cop-out. I'll give you a good example.

Ruth and I lived in an historical house in downtown Dayton for 24 years. It was in a somewhat distressed condition when we bought it, but it had been gutted and all new wiring, plumbing and mechanical systems installed. It was a real find — in a professional neighborhood, the location was central to our professional and social activities and the price was right. It turned out to be a great place for us!

Upon retirement, our boaters' dream was to live on the water. So, we bought a lot on Lake Erie in Marblehead, Ohio and began building our "dream-home-on-a-budget."

When we finally decided to retire and broke away from our business connections in Dayton we made preparations to sell our historic Dayton home. We repainted inside and out, installed new carpeting and updated some fixtures. In the process we made a surprising discovery!

There was a pass-through bar from the kitchen to the great room. There were bar stools on the great room side that were never used. (Isn't it interesting that we sometimes build in features we never use?)

When we pulled up the old great room carpeting, we found a damp, soft spot in the floor at the base of the pass-through. Wow! "Where is the water coming from?" I asked. I cut an opening in the floor and found that the floor cavity was also damp, but there was no obvious source of the water. There was a sink cabinet on the other side of the pass-through. I removed the bottom shelf of the cabinet. The floor was wet, but there was still no sign of a leak. I removed a section of drywall at the rear of the sink cabinet and found a leak in a copper water supply line joint.

It turned out to be a "dry joint" — which happens when a plumber misses a joint during the soldering process. The plumbing in this house had been completed over 30 years ago! This joint apparently had a very snug fit and didn't pull apart when the system was tested under pressure. But, it was not snug enough to be totally water tight. It was leaking about one drop of water every minute or two. Over the years evaporation helped hide the problem; no leakage was visible. But, there was enough residual water to create a problem in the floor, under the carpet, that also was not visible. Interestingly, the unfinished basement below did not show the signs of leakage either. The original wood floors had been covered with sheathing prior to carpeting and the extra thickness kept the moisture from showing through underneath.

I soldered the joint and then made repairs to the floor, the drywall and the sink cabinet. It was now better than new and we were ready for the new carpet.

Imagine! This was a home inspector's house. Shame on me for not knowing, right? I don't think so. I wouldn't tell this story just to embarrass myself. I tell it to prove that, like all other home inspectors, I don't have X-ray eyes or a crystal ball. Had I been inspecting this house, I certainly would not have identified the problem. Heck, I lived in this house for 24 years and had not seen any evidence of the problem!

**BOTTOM LINE: Unfortunately, I likely have inadvertently missed things that were not readily apparent in other houses over the years. Home inspectors do not engage in destructive investigation or testing. Therefore, we are not, nor can we be perfect.**

# A Christmas to Remember

It was an unusually cold, wet December. I arrived at my first house of the day; it was up on a hill. The long driveway was snow covered, so I would have to lug my ladder and tools up through the snow, take off my boots, and put on a clean pair of shoes and booties before entering the house. What a pain!

The roof was buried beneath the snow so I couldn't inspect it. Under these conditions my policy was to return and finish the inspection once the snow cleared.

I did another house in the afternoon; ditto on the snow. This continued for days. One snow covered roof after another until I had 12 houses on the incomplete list. Clients were calling and anxious, real estate agents were calling because I was holding up the works.

Finally, we had a thaw two days before Christmas. If we didn't get any more snow, it looked promising that the roofs on the list would be clear of snow the day before Christmas. That would work because I had planned not to work on Christmas Eve. This could be my catch-up opportunity!

December 24th arrived and I was out of bed at 4 AM to see if there had been any snow overnight. Not a flake had fallen; the roofs would be clear! Okay! Ruth volunteered to help me. We plotted the most efficient inspection sequence, and arrived at the first property just as the sun was coming up. Still some pockets of snow on the roof but we could still "git-er-done."

I took the ladder off the truck, positioned it, scrambled up, walked the roof, and inspected the shingles, the valleys, the caps, the penetrations, the flashings, and the chimney. I tried to take notes but my ballpoint wouldn't write — too cold. I called down to Ruth to roll down her window and take notes. I got off the roof, collapsed my ladder, secured it onto the roof rack and we hurried to the next house. Ruth was composing the report for the first house along the way. She read it to me; I tweaked it and she began her "ready-to-finalize" stack. Once we got home she would have to type all the addendum roof reports and fax them to clients.

Ditto on the snow and inspection process for the second house; only 10 more to go! At least I could get warmed up in the car between houses! Lunch was out of the question — too much to do! We'd broil a couple of big steaks when we got home!

Some of the remaining houses had patches of snow and ice; I just worked around them, breaking a cardinal rule of our profession — never put yourself in harm's way by walking on a wet, slippery roof! But we were making good progress and we were running out of time.

As I went from rooftop to rooftop all over town on Christmas Eve, it reminded me of old St Nick. I didn't have any reindeer but after all, my name is "Rudolph" and I did have "deer" Ruth!

It was getting late and the sun would be setting soon. We pressed on! It was now twilight; I would have to use my trusty flashlight to inspect the remaining roofs.

The last couple of houses were a real challenge. It was now dark, cold and miserable. I was cold, numb and dog tired. We kept going.

Finally we finished the last roof! It was way past dinnertime and we were too tired to cook, so we decided we would stop for a burger on the way home. Oops, almost forgot, it's Christmas Eve — everything was closed!

We went home and I built a fire in the fireplace. Ruth headed for her computer. "No," I said, "let's just relax. Nobody will be reading inspection reports on Christmas Eve or Christmas day. We'll just be sure to have them all ready to go the first thing in the morning the day after Christmas.

Let's have ourselves a merry little Christmas, Ruth!" "Merry Christmas, Rudy! How does hot buttered rum sound?" It was definitely too late to eat the big steaks we had looked forward to all day. "Hot buttered rum and a cheese plate sound fantastic!" Yes, it was definitely a Christmas to remember!

**BOTTOM LINE: Successful small business people get the job done, no matter what it takes!**


# Some Things Never Change

Over the years, I have inspected a number of houses two or more times; I even inspected one property four different times! After all, the population of my primary market was only about one million, so it was bound to happen.

One in particular, which I inspected it three times, stands out in my mind.

It had an attached garage that could compete with the Leaning Tower of Pisa. The top of the garage door opening had a slope of about 10 degrees — that's a lot! It was a classic case of differential settlement — where one part of a structure settles more than the remaining structure. It didn't take a crystal ball to spot this defect.

I had written this up on two previous inspections and I reported it again as an "area of concern". Why hadn't it been corrected? Maybe because the house was in a super-hot school district and houses were scarce? Did education trump defects? Perhaps because it was 50 years old the buyers thought this was part of the patina! Hell, I don't know what went through my clients' minds! After all, I'm not a shrink and it's none of my business anyway!

**BOTTOM LINE: Never practice psychoanalysis without a license! Just carefully and objectively report the defects and move on.**


# Some People Never Do Dishes

I always ask for permission before running a dishwasher. The seller was not home so I asked the listing agent, who saw no problem with my operating it. I learned to always look inside first — at one house the potato chips were stored there! I've also seen other things including dog treats and ladies underwear! This one was empty so I started it. A flood of water gushed out from under the unit! The agent was shocked; this defect had not been disclosed! She was kind enough to help me clean up the mess.

Some sellers obviously don't know what components are included in a professional home inspection. I checked dishwashers for proper function because they are permanently installed equipment. I also checked refrigerators and ranges, even though they are not permanently installed. If these appliances were transferring to the buyers, I felt an obligation to make sure they were functional.

**BOTTOM LINE: Buyers, sellers, real estate professionals and wannabe home inspectors can all benefit from knowing what constitutes a professional home inspection. That's one of the reasons for this book.**

# Repair Costs Exceeded the Value of the Home

An attorney from an adjoining state called. He was representing a young couple who had bought an older house only forced to move out of it two years later due to all the major problems that had developed. The house was "falling apart", he told me! His clients were suing the home inspector they had hired to inspect the property, the real estate agent who had recommended him, and the sellers. My interest was piqued! We made arrangements for a site visit.

As we drove up the lane, I could tell at first glance that the house was indeed in an advanced state of distress. The overhead garage door was grotesquely tilted in its out-of-square frame. The roof's ridgeline reminded me of a roller coaster. And cracks in the brick veneer wall cladding were clearly visible — even without getting out of my truck.

Inside, the floors were tilted precariously, the ceilings and walls were severely cracked and doors would not close. I asked where the basement stairs were so I could get some clues as to what was going on. "They are over here but you can't get down there!" I was told, "It's full of water." I approached the stairwell with the owner and the attorney and could not believe my eyes — I pulled out my tape measure and lowered it to the basement floor. The basement was actually full of six feet of standing water!

Although the structure could possibly be restored, repair costs would most likely far exceed the value of the home. Demolition loomed as the practical option.

What caused the damage and was the home inspector personally liable for not predicting it? The short answer is that without a doubt, this property had a serious flaw at the time of purchase and the home inspector did not alert his clients to it.

The house was over 40 years old, a modest wood framed structure built over a basement with poured concrete walls. Style and construction quality were both consistent with the era during which it was built. But the builder missed something very big. The house was built near the center of a large rural lot, on a site lower than the surrounding area. In other words, the house was built in a hole. To compound the issue, the top of the foundation was placed very low to the original grade level in order to give the house a popular low profile, California ranch appearance. As a result, the house had no doubt experienced a long history of basement flooding and settlement due to the constant wetting and erosion of the supporting soil under the foundation. The wall and ceiling cracks appeared to have been patched many times over the years. And the floors were no doubt becoming increasingly tilted over time as well.

Based upon what I observed, I concluded that it was highly probable that the foundation, while initially settling gradually over the years, had finally lost significant support from the underlying soil and experienced a rather sudden and dramatic downward movement. This caused the major damage, prompting the owners to move out. The attorney and the owners agreed that this was consistent with what the owners experienced.

The home inspector's report said nothing about the grading and drainage deficiencies. His report did not discuss evidence of any past flooding. And, it made no mention of the many cracks inside and outside the house. There were major foundation cracks which showed evidence of prior caulking; they were not mentioned either. I was incredulous. While home inspectors cannot be expected to have X-ray vision or a crystal ball, it was clear to me that this inspector should have seen and called attention to the visual evidence at hand and even recommended opinions from specialists, e.g. a structural and/or geotechnical engineer. He did not. While his report called out some minor deferred maintenance items, there was no mention of the serious problems presumably existing at this property.

Although this case had been in litigation for some time, the inspector's insurance company settled the claim for the cost of the house after receiving my field report. But sadly, even though the young couple received a favorable settlement, they had been put through hell. Several questions remain in my mind:

1. How could this inspector, who reportedly had been inspecting houses for twenty years, possibly miss the major issues at this property?
2. What, if anything, was going on between the inspector and the real estate agent, who "used him all the time?"
3. How did this inspector obtain a license to practice under the state's licensing law? Perhaps a flawed grandfathering provision based only on prior experience?

**BOTTOM LINE: I'm a devoted advocate of pre-purchase home inspections. But unfortunately all home inspectors are not created equal. Certified members of the American Society of Home Inspectors (ASHI) have had to demonstrate the highest levels of education and experience in the industry and, in my opinion, should receive first consideration. Do not hire anyone blindly. Ask about professional affiliations. Check with the Better Business Bureau. Ask about training and experience. Stay away from inspectors who compete solely on price. And be wary of those referred by real estate agents who recommend them "all the time."**

# How Did They Die?

The house was approximately 45 years old, vacant and in an estate; it had the original forced-air gas furnace. I found that the furnace had been improperly installed, creating a very serious safety situation which was dangerous and had not been corrected over the years.

The heavy scorch stains above the draft hood indicated that most, if not all of the exhaust gas was back-drafting into the basement and thence into the living space above. It was incredulous that this situation could have existed over the years without someone discovering and correcting it.

I advised the real estate agent representing the executor of the estate that this was a very serious problem. She responded, "That's ridiculous; these people lived here for 45 years and never had a problem."

Sensing she may have known the family, I asked her how many children had been raised in the house and how old they were now. She replied that there were three and that all had attended college and now had families of their own.

As I thought about this situation, I conjured up images of a young, active family bringing fresh air into the house every time entry doors were opened and closed. The original windows, which given the age and style of the house were notoriously leaky steel casement types, also allowed fresh air to enter. They had recently been replaced.

Then I asked the agent if she knew how the couple died. The wife had passed away a couple of years before her husband's recent death — both of natural causes. I drew no conclusions out loud but the scary scenario of a house filled with carbon monoxide, and no longer being diluted by outside air haunted me.

The kids left the nest. The parents tightened up the house for energy savings. Older people living in a death trap!

**Bottom Line: These people died of natural causes? I still wonder.........**

# The Cosmetic Powder Room

It was a nice, older home with many updates.  A recently completed powder room, created by converting a large closet in the foyer, was beautiful!  It was masterfully decorated with beautiful fixtures, luxurious towels and stunning wall treatments.

As I proceeded to inspect it, I was shocked to find that neither the sink nor toilet had any water supply or drain lines!  My clients were surprised and chagrined that no mention had been made of this.  The new powder room looked great but it was definitely not functional!

**BOTTOM LINE:  Even the most attractive renovation deserves a careful inspection.**


# The Big Leap

It was another jury trial.  Let me digress; I categorically don't much like them. They are expensive and the "right" parties don't always win.  Reasonable people, along with practical, hardworking attorneys and qualified technical support specialists should be able to settle most cases out of court, in my humble opinion.

I was on the stand being cross examined by the opposing attorney, a real bull dog and mental gymnast.  During his interrogation, he asked me a "yes" or "no" question which I perceived as a trap.  (Not unlike the old one about "When did you stop beating your wife?")  I replied, "Well, yes and no."  He declared that it was a simple question and again asked me in a demanding tone to answer "Yes or No."  I told him it was not that simple and that depending on the circumstances it could be answered either "yes or no". He turned and asked the judge for permission to approach the bench.  Both attorneys went forward for a brief sidebar discussion.

(At this point it's important to note that this trial had been on-going for nearly a week.  It was Friday afternoon and the judge was trying to hurry it along and wrap it up before the weekend.  He was obviously not in a very good mood.)

After their conversation, the judge addressed me.  "Mr. Platzer, I have determined that you *can* answer this question 'yes or no.' and, if you don't answer it 'yes or no,' I will consider holding you in contempt of court.  Do you understand?"  "Yes, your honor," I replied.

The attorney then repeated the question and then said very sternly, "Please answer yes or no, Mr. Platzer."  I paused for a reflective nanosecond, which felt like an eternity.  I looked at the jury, sheepishly shrugged my shoulders and said, "yes or no." And then in another nanosecond I caught the judge out of the corner of my eye.  Before the judge could speak, the attorney quickly announced, "Your honor, I withdraw the question, and I have no further questions for this witness."

I had established good visual rapport with the jury and had this attorney let the judge send me to jail, he would have suffered a big loss with them.  After all, I was just trying to be truthful and precise.  And, he was badgering me!

The judge didn't have to mete out disruptive discipline, and I had sabotaged the attorney's line of questioning, a very big leap indeed!

**BOTTOM LINE:  A tip for you home inspectors out there who do expert witnessing. I would highly recommend you not try this maneuver on your own.  You may not be as lucky as I was.  Bread and water – aarggggggg!**

# Too Much Attention to Detail

I was inspecting a chimney on a two-story roof. It was at the end of the house and I had a good view of the brickwork on its inward facing side. But, I couldn't get a good view of the outside. I extended myself around the chimney to get a better look when I lost my balance and fell to the one-story garage roof below.

I was lucky enough to fall parallel and between two roof trusses where the plywood decking provided somewhat of a trampoline effect. Still, it knocked the wind out of me and I thought for sure I was a goner. After several agonizing seconds, which seemed like an eternity, I was again able to breathe. I checked myself over for any damaged or missing parts and fortunately found none to be defective! Now I had another problem. My 32' extension ladder was at the two-story roof and I was now on a one-story roof. I called to the elderly seller and asked her if by chance she had a tall step ladder. She went in the garage and returned with a rickety old wooden ladder that I was able to use to get down to terra firma.

**BOTTOM LINE: A home inspector's job definitely has its ups and downs.**


# The House with Personality

It was a 1920 something mansion. The buyer was an executive transferring in from another state. He wanted a house in this neighborhood because it was reputed to have the finest school system in the greater metropolitan area.

The structure was Tudor-style and very original. In this case "original" meant the basic elements of the house had not been updated or replaced. There was no insulation, the steel casement windows were not in good repair, the original steam boiler, encased in asbestos insulation, was still chugging away inefficiently, and the plumbing and electrical systems were totally outdated. But from the street the house was charming and it was impeccably decorated inside as well.

My report would be detailed as usual, and would contain a number of updating recommendations. One of the things I targeted was the plumbing system. It had a lead water service line from the street, which needless to say had to be replaced! The water supply lines were galvanized steel, were clogged with rust and were firm candidates for replacement. I demonstrated why this was needed to my client. The shower on the third floor produced only a trickle of water and when I turned on any other faucet in the house there was absolutely no flow of water from the shower head. The listing real estate agent overheard my conversation and asked if he could have a word with me.

We went outside where he explained to me that "This house has personality! You've got to go easy on old houses like this." I told him I would leave the "personality" assessment to him and that he was barking up the wrong tree if he expected me to overlook a plumbing system that was clearly in failure.

The agent and I had a continuing strained relationship over the years. I guess you could call it a "personality" conflict.

**BOTTOM LINE: I've lived in old houses, I've restored and renovated old houses and I too, love their "personality". Just like choosing a spouse, don't let personality be the only criterion for making a good decision! In the case of a house, get a home inspection from a professional who will see beyond the personality.**

# Low Test Scores

Ruth and I were both certified EPA and state licensed radon testers. Radon is a naturally occurring, radioactive gas emitted from rocks deep within the earth. It occurs in varying amounts across the continent. The EPA has determined that if air is contaminated by the gas, at a level at or above a radioactive measure of 4 picocuries per liter of air, it is a health hazard which should be remediated.

We inspected houses for radon in conjunction with our home inspections as an additional service to our clients who requested it. One radon test we did caused us to re-evaluate whether we wanted to continue to provide that service.

My client was a super-savvy home buyer who had done his homework on buying a house. He interviewed several inspectors over the phone before hiring me to inspect the house he intended to buy. I liked that kind of client! I inspected the house, finding some minor issues, but nothing that would break the bank for either him or the sellers. I set up the radon detection equipment, leaving detailed instructions for the occupants about the protocols necessary for them to follow while the testing was underway. They were supposed to keep all windows closed for the duration of the test, and doors as well, except for normal entry and exit.

We picked up our detection equipment two days later, performed an analysis of the data recorded which determined the radon level within the house was substantially below the 4 picocurie level.

It is important to note that radon levels can vary widely from hour-to-hour, day-to-day and season-to-season, yet the standard test for a real estate transaction is only 48 hours. So, as part of our service we offered to provide at our cost, a passive, long-term radon detector which could be hung in an inconspicuous place and provide radon data over a period of 6 to 12 months.

This client, who had four school aged children, gratefully accepted our offer of this long-term test. A year later he delivered the detection device to us and we sent it to the laboratory for analysis. The results were alarming! They showed an excessively high average radon level over the protracted testing period. My client was very disappointed and he was very concerned.

I explained how we meticulously followed the calibration protocols for our testing devices and again explained the limitation of the 48 hour testing. He understood but was not satisfied.

I asked if he had developed any relationships in the neighborhood. He said his wife had befriended a neighbor over the back fence. I suggested that this neighbor might be a source of information about the situation.

He called me several days later. His wife had talked to the neighbor, who related that the seller had confided in her that she knew everything about radon testing. She went on to boast that she had kept all her doors open during the testing period to ventilate the house. This occurrence was enough for me to decide that I no longer wanted to be involved in a process which included critical elements over which I had no control.

**BOTTOM LINE: Home buyers should realize that while a high reading from a short-term test is useful to identify a need for remediation, a low reading from a 48 hour radon test is not necessarily reliable. It can be invalidated if the testing protocols are not followed by the occupants or if emissions happen to be unusually low during that 48 hour testing period. In these cases, only long-term testing can produce reliable results.**

# A Cell Phone Problem

Some folks have problems with their cell phones; they get outside of their coverage area, they experience dropped calls, their battery dies, they occasionally misplace their phone and have to call it on a land-line to find it, etc. Home inspectors experience the same things and then some.

I once drowned my cell phone as it went jumped in while I doing a ph test on a swimming pool! I dropped another one somewhere in an attic full of blown-in insulation and I never could find it. One came out of my pocket while on a roof and I helplessly watched as it slid down the steep slope, flew over the rain gutter and made a crash landing on the driveway. On another roof I lost control of my phone and it too slid down the roof, but this time it landed in the rain gutter. "At least I didn't lose this one", I thought. Wrong! The gutter was full of water! Wrote that up!

**BOTTOM LINE: More stories about the life of an intrepid (clumsy) home inspector. Ah, the good old days! Now, fortunately, we have all ways of securing these vital little suckers to our personages. And, I remember what it was like to have to leave the inspection site to go and find a pay phone so, yes, I do say they are vital.**

# A Flood Waiting to Happen

My dentist's assistant told me that she was buying her first house. And because her husband was deployed to Iraq, she was taking care of everything herself. It was an exciting yet daunting task. I asked if she was having the house inspected, and she said they couldn't really afford to do so. I offered to take a look free of charge; she was elated. It was a new, two story house with a walk-out basement.

As soon as I arrived I saw a big problem! Her lot was at the bottom of a long incline with the entire plat of homes stretching out to a much higher level. There was a drainage ditch at the rear of the lot to manage all of the run-off and divert it to a large drain tile under the street.

As I stood there looking up the hill, I could imagine the river of water running through this gulley during a heavy spring rain. I feared the drain tile would not be able to handle it and her basement family room would be flooded! My client took this information to the project superintendent. He told her I was "nuts."

So, I called a licensed, PhD geotechnical engineer with whom I had worked on several legal cases. I told him about the young military couple and he volunteered to meet me at the site (also without charge).

When he arrived, he simply shook his head; he agreed with my assessment wholeheartedly and wrote a letter to that effect.

Our client was disappointed but also relieved that she had not closed on a problem house. The builder reluctantly refunded her earnest money.

A few weeks later she called to say she had found another new house in a nearby plat. She was understandably anxious until the completion of the inspection — that one passed muster!

**BOTTOM LINE: One more time — every new house needs to be inspected! If you think you cannot afford an inspection; you also cannot afford to deal with unforeseen problems.**

# Is It True?

Radon is a radioactive gas that can't be seen, smelled or tasted. It is a by-product of the breakdown of uranium in soil and rocks. Radon is found all over the US, in greater or lesser amounts. As radon escapes from the soil, it mixes with the air we breathe. The EPA estimates some 20,000 lung cancer deaths a year are caused by radon. The risk of exposure is greater inside homes and office buildings where it gets trapped and builds to higher levels of concentration. But, believe it or not, some home buyers, home owners and real estate professionals discount or ignore the radon threat!

When clients asked me about radon testing I told them the story of our cat. He was strictly an indoor cat, spending the last 10 years of his life in our house 24/7. Both Ruth and I worked, so we spent a lot less time at home than he did.

When we decided to offer radon testing to our home inspection clients, both Ruth and I took the required EPA training and became licensed radon testers. The coursework really opened our eyes. Radon was real and it was dangerous. The first house we tested was our own. The average radon level was nearly five times the level at which the EPA recommends mitigation. We immediately installed a mitigation system which reduced the average level in our house to about the level found outdoors.

But what does this have to do with the cat? Well, after 10 years of exposure in our house, he died of lung cancer. Was this a coincidence? Maybe, but we couldn't rule out the possibility that he, as well as we, lived in a virtual death trap! Hummmmmmmm.

**BOTTOM LINE: Do you believe in radon? Should you have your house tested?**

# In Search of the Perfect House

It wasn't a "bad" house. It had a few minor issues which could have been easily fixed. And the seller would have, more than likely, taken care of them if asked to do so.

My client was a young engineer and a first time home buyer, and he was disappointed. He expected more. Even though I explained the house had no major problems and was average or perhaps a little above average for its age group, he decided not to buy it.

A couple of weeks later we met again at another property. He expressed his delight that this house was by far better than the first. Well, my inspection confirmed that the imperfections I identified in the first house were not present in this one. But, guess what? There were other issues, including one that would be costly to correct. The client made an almost immediate decision to discard this house and the air was thick with disappointment.

Almost a week later, I inspected yet a third house for this client. When we met at the property I tried to paint a happy face on the situation by quipping, "We've got to stop meeting like this." It was not received in the same lighthearted way in which it was intended. The client explained that he was now somewhat panicked to find a house. His wife wanted to get settled in before school and wanted to be in this school district. And, you guessed it; the beginning of the school year was now just around the corner. He was anxious to get on with the inspection.

Well, the punch line is that this house was the worst of the three. It was not in good repair. And, you guessed it, he bought it anyway! The worst of the three! How could this happen? Was I in some way responsible? I learned a big lesson from this experience regarding clients who are looking for the perfect house. I had thought my job was to inspect houses. Now I realized that my job was to help people buy houses.

After this experience, I started telling people who were picking apart good properties "There is no such thing as a perfect house. I've never built one, inspected one or even seen one! They just don't exist!" I told clients who were disappointed over minor issues that yes, A, B and C in this house needed attention. But, if you reject this house and find another house without A, B and C as issues, it is highly possible that it will have minor D, E and F issues, because, "there are no perfect houses."

**BOTTOM LINE: Unfortunately, over the years, I had a few other similar experiences. Maybe clients thought I was trying to "sell" them on the house. I hope not, but it is possible. This raises another good point. The bond of trust between an inspector and the client is crucial to a successful inspection.**

# Let's Get the Story Straight

A lawyer asked me to look at a house with a serious water intrusion problem. His clients — the owners — bought the house a year earlier and had just experienced a flood in their newly finished basement family room two days ago.

The house was in a rural area. As I drove up to the property, I noticed a drainage ditch and a culvert under the driveway, which is not unusual in that setting. What puzzled me, however, was the water running through the ditch. We were in the midst of a prolonged drought and I fleetingly wondered about the source of this water.

The basement had indeed flooded; there was evidence on the floor and lower wall areas, along with a substantial amount of damage. The owners said that they were told by the sellers about a previous water problem, which had been fixed. They showed me an invoice from a basement water-proofing contractor who had installed an expensive perimeter drainage system. The sellers had claimed that after two years, they had no further problems. But, "The problem was obviously not fixed!" the owners insisted. They had put pieces of duct tape at locations along the wall where "water had come through." I tested these areas with an electronic moisture meter and they tested dry. After only two days, they would have tested damp, had this been the case.

I reviewed the exposed part of the drainage system — not one, but two sump pits and two pumps. One appeared to be the primary and the other a back-up. Both pumps were functional. The primary pump was operating every couple of minutes. The water entering the sumps was clear and cold.

I went outside — grading around the foundation appeared adequate; I saw no problems with the roof drainage system. I went back to the drainage ditch beside the road — there was plant growth and algae in the water. It was starting to make sense — ground water. Underground streams and springs are not unusual in this area. While I couldn't offer an opinion as to the source of the water, I concluded that this basement was receiving a constant flow of water from under or around the foundation and that if the two pumps quit working, there would be a flood. Without a secondary power source, such as an auxiliary generator, an electric power outage would pose a big problem. The house had no such generator, nor did it have emergency 12-volt back-up pumps. I reported back to the attorney that, in my opinion, the water came from overflowing sump pits, probably due to a power outage.

**BOTTOM LINE: Did the owners have a case?**

# ANNEX -- SOME THINGS TO PONDER

## Tips on Selecting a House

"Location, location, location," as the saying goes, is the number one criterion for selecting a house according to real estate professionals. It is highly important, but not the only consideration. There are many other factors to consider.

You <u>pay</u> for location. A house on one side of town can cost twice or three times as much as a house of equal size, construction and condition on the other side of town. The quality of the schools and services, proximity to major thoroughfares and shopping, as well as neighborhood cultural differences can all make a big difference. Newer areas generally command higher prices, all other things being equal. Older neighborhoods can have bargains, especially if there are signs of urban revival, but schools and services may be less than optimal. So, it's decision time. Buyers should carefully sort through their priorities and budgets as the first order of business when looking for a house. Why waste time in a neighborhood that's too expensive, or looking for a bargain in a location that's too short on services. Do your homework on neighborhoods!

Now, let's discuss by general category the type of houses that are out there. We'll begin with the various types of **New Construction**:

**Plat Homes,** or "cookie cutter" houses (similar designs) are quite popular. They are planned developments that frequently incorporate open spaces, parks, clubhouses, pools, etc. and spur the growth of nearby shopping and service companies.

There are good developers and some not so good. The quality of the homes they build can vary greatly from one to another. But, you say, "They're all inspected by code inspection officials, aren't they?" Yes and no. Some areas still don't have building codes! Moreover, a building code is but a <u>minimum </u>construction standard. And codes vary from one administrative jurisdiction to another. Code enforcement varies also. And unfortunately, code inspectors are often over-worked and underpaid.

So, how do you know what kind of house you're getting? Have it inspected by a qualified, professional, independent home inspector. Time and time again I hear real estate agents telling their customers, "This is a new home, why would you spend the money to have it inspected?"

Well, when I drive up to inspect a new home, I don't have a clue as to what I might find, but I know I'll find something – often something big. Clients will ask, "How could the builder have missed it?" "How could the code inspector have missed it?" The answer is quite simple. People aren't perfect, builders aren't perfect, sub-contractors aren't perfect, and code inspectors aren't perfect. A professional home inspector, by virtue of training and experience, knows what deficiencies to look for and provides a valuable service to yes, even new home buyers. Once identified, the builder will usually correct these mistakes, and enlightened builders may even learn a lesson in the process. It might even help them avoid future law suits. It is definitely a win-win situation.

Let me emphasize one more time, HAVE YOUR NEW HOUSE INSPECTED.

**Custom Homes**, in my experience, have a much greater potential for huge mistakes than plat homes! I call custom homes "Research and Development Houses." By definition, they are one-of-a-kind, and never built before. Cookie cutter houses are built the same every time. Workmen get used to building them and builders learn from their mistakes as they build more. A custom home is entirely different. It takes better design and planning, more astute general contracting and highly qualified workers. I have inspected a number of them, and provide examples of things I've found throughout this book. I have also worked with attorneys on numerous law suits against custom home builders. Some of these turn out to be "houses from hell." What a shame. Had these houses been inspected by qualified inspectors during construction, some of these suits could have been avoided. And owners wouldn't be faced with the trauma and expense of trying to get major problems corrected. Moreover, inept builders wouldn't be learning the hard way, through painful and expensive law suits.

Now let's look at houses by age groups.

## Houses Under Ten Years Old are starting to develop a track record. They've been around long enough to be exhibiting signs of any major problems.

For example, when inspecting a new house we expect to find a good foundation (not always). But a ten year old foundation has had a chance to settle and can exhibit clues as to what kind of soil, drainage or construction problems might be rearing their ugly heads. We can also see tell-tale signs of developing problems with roofing, siding, concrete floor slabs, patios, windows, decks, doors, driveways and walks. The same goes for wall and ceiling cracks, door and window alignments, leak stains, etc.

While most of these elements are usually found to be aging well, the average roof has used up a significant portion of its life expectancy. The water heater and dishwasher will need to be replaced soon, if they haven't been already, the "builder quality" insulating glass window panels may be starting to "fog" due to broken seals, exterior paint and caulking may be needed, etc..

A good home inspector will assess the condition of these and many other items, provide life expectancy information, discuss needed repairs and make preventive maintenance recommendations. Do I need to say more? Have that house professionally inspected!

Now let's examine **Older Houses**. Real estate agents like to use the term "older". This can mean they don't know how old a house is or they don't want you to know how old it is.

## Twenty Something houses are far beyond the first round of appliance replacements. Some will be close to second-time replacement. Many will need a new roof now or very soon. And some will have deferred maintenance items neglected over the years. In addition, they may have developed grading and drainage problems. Concrete flatwork may be deteriorating. Plumbing fixtures may be at or near their normal life expectancy. Furnaces are starting to be questionable in terms of safety and efficiency. And air conditioners that have lasted this long are now on borrowed time. Insulation may not meet the model energy code of the day.

Some of these houses will have been well built and well maintained with replacements made before becoming problems, and are a joy to inspect.
But don't be too quick to judge a book by its cover. A twenty year old house may have had a cosmetic make-over. The real estate agent may point out "the newer, neutral carpeting, fresh paint, updated light fixtures, etc." — all the things that a home inspector

couldn't care less about. A twenty-something house bears close scrutiny by, you guessed it, a professional home inspector.

## Thirty-Year And Beyond Houses can be a challenge for the home inspector.

They become a mix of various aged components, some of which have overtaken their normal life expectancy, are terribly inefficient or have established a track record of serious problems or hazards. Many of these houses will be of basically good construction and be worthy of the upgrades needed to make them very comfortable. The advice and recommendations a seasoned home inspector can provide on homes in this age group can be invaluable!

## Houses 50 Or More Years Old tend to be a real mixed bag. Most of these houses

have experienced some level of remodeling and some even have newer additions. The major systems — plumbing, electrical, heating, air conditioning, roof, siding, etc. need extra careful evaluation. Some may be original and overdue for upgrade or replacement. Many will have undergone repairs or updating over the years.

There are many repair people, including remodeling contractors, roofers, plumbers, etc. who perform good work and perhaps just as many others who don't have a clue! And then there are the do-it-yourself weekend warriors, who do some amazingly dumb things to houses. I have included some examples in this book. I charged more for doing houses over 50 years old because they take longer to inspect and demand more discussion with clients.

## Ancient Houses, let's say 75 years and older, have survived the test of time. I've

inspected some built in the late Eighteenth Century! These houses have survived for a reason. They were built well to begin with, and have been protected from water intrusion (the number one killer of old structures) and they have been effectively maintained and carefully updated.

One 1802 farmhouse comes to mind, that was a real treat to inspect. It had some problems, but with one major and a few minor repairs would be a very comfortable place to live. And just imagine the history occupants would be surrounded by every day!

There is a certain group of people who buy "fixer-upper" old houses to restore. Most of these tend to be good, solid people with high hopes of bringing an ancient house back to life. I have a special place in my heart for these folks because I've been there and done that. What an experience!

People who consider buying these houses need a pre-purchase inspection perhaps more than anyone else. The cast iron, claw-foot bathtub is in great shape, but the plumbing system it's hooked up to might be an absolute mess and in need of replacement. The old lighting fixtures can be restored rather inexpensively, but the whole house might need a new electrical system. Yes, it will need a new heating system, but removing an asbestos-clad boiler and heating pipes will be the most expensive part of that replacement. All of the windows and exterior doors may need extensive repair or replacement. The plaster walls and ceilings will probably require a lot of work. And it usually goes on and on once the work begins. My hat is off to those who restore the homes that are a part of our national heritage but the personal commitment, hard work and expense can be far more than ever imagined. Find a home inspector with this kind of experience before you buy. You'll be forever grateful you did!

**BOTTOM LINE: When buying a home, knowledge up front can be a huge money saver in the future!**

# Making Rational Versus Emotional Decisions

I inspected homes for thousands of good people over my twenty five years of practice and I was amazed by how many of them allowed their emotions to control their buying decisions.

Real estate agents know this; read their listing descriptions. They use words like "charming, inviting, comfortable, beautiful, unique, updated" — and these descriptors may well be appropriate. But they elicit an emotional rather than an objective, rational response. "Isn't this a cute room?" "Can't you just see your family in front of this fireplace on Christmas Eve?" "Wouldn't this floor plan be excellent for entertaining?"

Unfortunately, such enticements leave a lot to be desired. They don't answer the many other questions that should be asked by savvy buyers — questions about the neighborhood, the schools, street traffic, and most importantly, from my perspective, the condition of the property.

Too often I had clients who had fallen in love with a house and hired me in hopes of my giving it a seal of approval. Wouldn't that be wonderful — a love affair that resulted in a "living happily ever after" ending?

I too, was optimistic that I could bless this union of a happy buyer and home. Nothing satisfied me more than to find that a buyer had chosen a nice, clean, well-maintained home! And it was always difficult for me when it became necessary to burst that bubble of anticipation. I may have found a major basement foundation or flooding problem, a bad roof, unsafe wiring, structural anomalies, or any number of other potential drawbacks. And I was obliged to disclose those findings to my clients. I always worked hard to put my findings in proper perspective for them. I explained that almost anything found wrong could be fixed and reminded them that typically, contracts to buy allow the buyer to ask that these defects be corrected by the seller. Then I stepped out of the picture, hoping that things would work out — that deficiencies would be corrected and my clients would not only get the house of their dreams, but also one which was safe and habitable. Not always!

Occasionally, I was called upon to inspect a property which I had inspected previously, and in which I had found and disclosed major defects. (If the prior client was still the owner, we always asked their permission to inspect the house for their potential buyer.) Incredibly, I sometimes found the same problems I had previously reported and asked myself, "What's going on here? Were they listening? Did they grasp what I'd said? Did they ignore my findings? Did they ask the sellers to fix the problems and did they declined to fix them? Did the buyer take on the responsibility of fixing the problems and then fail to do so?" Or, were problems overlooked because of an emotional attachment to the property?

In my view the answer often was that emotion trumped rationality. Emotion won over reason. Nothing else was on their radar. Now, guess what? My new client had the same right to ask that the problems be remedied by my former client. What went around came back around!

**BOTTOM LINE: My experience tells me that strictly emotional decisions are not helpful when choosing a house. So, at least hire a home inspector; get the facts and use them to help you make the right decision. And when defects are disclosed, have them corrected for your own safety and peace of mind — and when it comes time to sell the property, the issues will be behind you.**

# Looking Ahead

**How Long Will This House Meet Your Needs?**  Planning in any context can be a difficult thing for some folks to do.  Most people are caught up in the process of dealing with today's issues and have little or no time or inclination to think about the future.

And so it is not surprising that many people think the same way when buying a house.  Many times people buy or build a house to accommodate today's requirements only.  They don't ask themselves about the future.

- ✓ How long do we intend to live in this house?
- ✓ How many children do we expect to have?
- ✓ Is a live-in relative a possibility in the future?
- ✓ Are we going to retire in this house?

These are just some of the questions you might ask to help determine your future requirements.

**Do You Really Like The House Or Do You Intend To Drastically Change It?**
Sometimes people overestimate the time they expect to stay in the house.  I often get first-time home buyers who ask numerous questions about making major improvements to the property.  "Can we remove this wall to open up the space between the kitchen and family room?"  "How much will it cost to enlarge the garage?"  "We're going to replace the windows and doors; what type do you recommend?"  These are some of the more popular ones asked.  I respond by asking them how long they expect to be in the house.  They usually say "for a long time, maybe forever."  I tell them that may be unrealistic.  Most people live in several houses during their lifetimes.

All the money they spend on improvements will hopefully make the house more comfortable for them and perhaps more desirable for the next owners, but probably won't increase the value very much, if any.  Homes are appraised based upon other like properties recently sold in the neighborhood.  If your single story, three-bedroom, one-and-a-half bath, ranch on a slab is identical in description to three other houses nearby sold in the past six months, your appraised value will probably nearly match those properties.  The fact that you put all the money in upgrades probably won't affect that appraisal.  I always advise my first time buyers to make only the unnecessary "nice-to-have" improvements that they think they can't live without, knowing that the payback will be in comfort and personal satisfaction, not in dollars and cents at resale.  Instead, I suggest they consider setting that money aside for the day when it's time to buy their real dream home!

**Is This A Retirement Home?**  There's another interesting phenomenon I experienced with respect to people nearing retirement age.  They were buying or building their dream home, and they have lived in enough houses over the years to know exactly what they want.  But is their dream home really a retirement home?  It might have two, or even three stories with no elevator, doors and hallways that are not wheelchair accessible, elevated decks or balconies with stairs, a hot tub and swimming pool and other things most older people don't need or won't use.  If well thought out, a real retirement home might be entirely different.  It might even include a home theatre, a hobby room or workshop and some other not-often-thought-of amenities such as mechanical systems which can be easily winterized or monitored during long vacations or visits to the kids' places.  A good architect or builder can be helpful in identifying retirement features, as can a knowledgeable home inspector.

**Where Is The Neighborhood Headed?** Another forward look should be taken at the neighborhood. Are property values going up or down in this area? Don't be too optimistic in your assessment. Some neighborhoods may look like they are coming back, but never quite make it. Those investments go down. On the other hand, some downtown properties are becoming more and more attractive to the Gen X crowd as well as others trying to escape the heavy traffic and long commutes from the suburbs. Some of these ram-shackle properties seem overpriced for what they are, but may be "no-brainers" as far as investment and appreciation are concerned. Just be sure you know the condition of the property and don't underestimate what will be required to bring it back. Yes, a professional home inspector can be your best friend in this scenario.

**What About Those Low Condo Fees?** There is a continuing trend toward condominium living as well, and for good reason. You just move in, pay for common maintenance costs, and live happily ever after, right? Well, maybe not. Maintenance fees are usually based on today's maintenance costs. As the buildings begin to wear out, the management fees will probably increase. And when new roofs, siding, painting, sidewalk and street repairs or other common area improvements or replacements become necessary, assessments may be made on all condo owners. This becomes necessary when the association does not have an adequate reserve fund built up over time to take care of these expenditures. And many condo associations are trying to keep their fees low and don't have adequate reserves.

**What About The Condo Association And Their Restrictions And Rules?** One other caution with respect to condos – be sure you know exactly what you are buying! I am aware of a development called a "boataminium." It is advertised as "lots with deeded docks." Would you be led to believe that this means you buy a lot and a dock that is also deeded? Most people think that is what they bought. In fact, what they bought is the right to put a manufactured double-wide home on a lot which is part of the common property of a mobile home park! Yes, they do own the dock and the land beneath it, but not the land their mobile home occupies. Many people who buy condos never read the governing rules of the association until it is too late. In the "boataminium" example cited above, under certain conditions, such as nonpayment of association fees, their mobile home can be removed from the common-area lot, at their expense.

Remember that along with the advantages of condominium living come restrictions on what you can and cannot do inside and outside of your unit. And you will have only one vote in the administration and management of the complex. Moreover, there is the unpredictable cost of increased management fees and assessments over time. There are advantages and disadvantages to most everything. Read the documents before you buy to know what you are buying.

**How Well Is The Condo Built?** Many people believe that it doesn't matter how well a condo is built because they are not responsible for maintaining it. Many condos, however, are built at a minimum quality level, and this will affect when repairs and replacements will become necessary. Also, determine the elements of the building for which you will be personally responsible. For example, window and door repairs are often the owner's responsibility, and this can become expensive.

**BOTTOM LINE: Know what you're buying! And above all, have a pre-purchase inspection by a professional independent home inspector, yes, even a condo!**

# Tips on Selecting a Custom Builder

I bet you've heard many people say that if you can survive building a house together you can survive anything! Yes, building a house is exciting but it is also very stressful, even under the best of circumstances! There are so many decisions to make — and all of them seem accompanied by both a sense of urgency and too many choices! Selecting the right builder can help ease some of the strain as well as ensure you get what you want as well as what you are paying for.

Who you select to build your house is the most important decision of the entire process. Unfortunately, many poorly informed people make this important decision using the wrong criteria.

I often hear comments like, "We met this builder at (fill in the blank — our church, country club, a party, etc.) and he is a great guy." or, "He's a friend of a friend. He took us to dinner, and he's very impressive." Or, "He's my son-in-law's father, he's like part of the family!" Folks who make this important decision based on anecdotal information could be headed for big trouble.

You need only talk to someone who has been through a home building nightmare to understand what I'm saying. Perhaps their builder went bankrupt half way through construction. He may have even drawn the money from their construction loan and used it to skip town! Maybe they got a finished house with major problems, some of which were nearly impossible to correct. In any new house with problems — emotional, legal and financial troubles are usually the result.

As a consultant to attorneys, I learned a great deal about contractors being sued for building bad houses. Most were well-meaning, "nice" guys. Some were inexperienced and lacked a track record of satisfied customers. Some were smooth talkers and better sales people than builders. Some called themselves "Custom Builders", but lacked the background, training and experience to undertake the management and supervision of a complex project like a custom home.

I recall two brothers who were air conditioning technicians and thought *that* experience qualified them to be general contractors. After all, they had worked in many new houses and thought, "How difficult can that builder's job be? We do all the work, he just shows up and looks around!" (I've seen that same mistake made by electricians, carpenters and other trades people who were well-qualified in their specialties but ill-equipped to build houses.) The first house these two brothers built ended up with a major problem which would cost tens of thousands of dollars to repair. As a result, they were forced into bankruptcy. And, unfortunately, that left the homeowners with both the repair bills and their attorney's fees — an all too common occurrence.

In another case, an experienced carpenter undertook the construction of a complex room addition. It included a huge indoor swimming pool which required a sophisticated heating, air-conditioning and ventilation system. Because that system did not perform properly, the enclosure was eaten up by mold. Moreover, the complicated roof structure was built with a significant roof framing defect and the roof ultimately collapsed. Luckily no one was in the room at the time! The entire structure required an expensive rebuild. Even though the builder was an experienced carpenter, the complexity of this project was well beyond his expertise. You guess it; he went bankrupt. And once again the homeowners were left with the heartache and the expense of rectifying the problems.

Another case involved a reputable builder's son with an MBA from an Ivy League school. When the father retired, he naturally put his son in charge. The new company president was surely well-schooled in accounting, finance, marketing, etc. but, he knew absolutely nothing about good building practices! His first house was a large custom home that ended up with several serious problems. The worst part of this particular case was that he couldn't even understand the defects or accept them as problems. Dad was undoubtedly very disappointed! So were the buyers!

Here's one more example. A builder with a good reputation for building production tract homes decided to venture out of his league to build a large, complicated, custom home. "Why not go after this market next?" he thought. Unfortunately, his first custom house turned out to be an absolute travesty — requiring a half million dollars in repairs to even make it safe and habitable. The homeowners literally lived a decade-long litigation and repair nightmare and no doubt had trouble ever again thinking of this place as their "dream" home.

The people who chose these contractors needed more information to help guide their selection process. And they would have benefitted from progress inspections by a qualified home inspector. Unfortunately, after the fact, they received plenty of information about bad builders — during the litigation process. And at a very high cost!

So what should you look for?

- Years of experience building houses of the type you are considering. Ask for a list of addresses and drive by them. How do they look compared to the houses built by others in the neighborhood?
- Credible recommendations from past customers with similar houses. Ask for the names, addresses and phone numbers of a couple of past clients and ask them about their experience. Would they use this builder again? Were there problems? How were they handled?
- A good record with the Better Business Bureau. Be sure the builder has no unresolved complaints. The BBB rates businesses; what is the builder's rating? Is it A+ or D?
- A good credit rating. The builder should be willing to give you a bank reference.
- A written contract reviewed by your attorney. How are decisions made? How are changes handled? How are disputes resolved?
- A detailed set of construction drawings preferably prepared or reviewed by an architect. Some people have told me that their builder said that plans were not really necessary. Build me a house "like that one" or "like this sketch I drew" is a sure-fire way to create problems. Detailed construction drawings ensure that you get what you want and that the builder understands what is required. Do your homework specifying the major systems too. An efficient furnace or water heater may be considered an "upgrade" by the builder unless it is specified on the plans.

One more bit of advice. Begin picking out plumbing and electrical fixtures, cabinets, flooring, etc. sooner rather than later. This will allow you to develop a realistic budget and to enjoy the process more.

**BOTTOM LINE: Don't let your dream house turn into a nightmare! Do your homework and make an investment in selecting the right people to help you up-front. It could save you big money in the long run.**

# Tips on Selecting a Real Estate Agent

In my experience, many people don't know how real estate agents function. So before you select one, here are some important things I believe you should understand.

The Rules of Traditional Real Estate.

First and foremost, the role of the traditional agent is to represent and serve the best interests of the <u>seller</u>, not the buyer! An agent who lists a property has a <u>legal obligation</u> to get the best deal for the <u>seller</u>, not the buyer!

For example:

Let's say you are being shown a house by "your" agent (who is really the seller's agent).

If you comment that you'd be willing to purchase the property for $240,000, the agent has an <u>obligation</u> to provide this information to the seller. And, "your" agent may already know that the seller would accept $230,000, but is not at liberty to tell you that! Read that again!

No, you insist, "My agent, Sue Jones, would never do that to me. Her mother has been a good friend of my family for years. I trust her!" Maybe so, but remember that Sue Jones has a <u>legal obligation to the seller</u>, not to you.

"But wait a minute," you remember, "Sue Jones doesn't even work for the real estate firm selling the house. The sign says ABC Realty and Sue works for XYZ Realty." Here is how it works: ABC Realty lists the property for sale and puts it on the Multiple Listing — a list of all the area properties for sale. By contractual agreement, any real estate agent from any other real estate firm can show the property on behalf of ABC Realty. So, when Sue shows you the property, she is doing so on behalf of (as an agent of) ABC Realty. As an agent of ABC, she shares their legal responsibility to get the best deal for the seller.

So when Sue "betrays" you to ABC Realty it is not because she is a bad person, she's just doing her job. You betrayed your own best interests by talking freely with and confiding in Sue.

So what's a poor buyer to do? Beyond guarded conversations with "your" real estate agent, there is another answer — hire a buyer's agent, often called a buyer broker.

The Role of the Buyer Broker.

Buyer brokers are real estate agents who choose to have a contractual agreement to represent <u>the buyer's</u> best interests. They do not list houses, so you'll never see their name on a "FOR SALE" sign. They work only for buyers.

How are these buyer brokers like traditional agents? They are both licensed real estate agents. They both are able to show any house listed on the Multiple Listing. And, they both can handle all the details and paperwork associated with financing, appraisal, closing, etc.

How are they different? They enter into an agreement with you, the buyer, to work in your best interests. They accept a payment from you (perhaps as low as $1) to make the agreement to represent your interests a binding contract. They are now legally bound to get you the best deal.

There's another big difference in how a buyer's agent operates. Let's go back to ABC Realty for a moment. They have a number of properties listed and a number of agents who would like to sell these properties. When they sell their own listings they keep all of the commissions. If they sell properties listed by other companies, they split the commissions with the other company. Because they are motivated to want to get the entire commission, they will want to show all their listings first — even if there are other properties on the Multiple Listing which might better satisfy your requirements.

A buyer broker doesn't have any listings, and therefore has no self-serving interest in showing you only certain properties. He or she can review all the properties listed on the Multiple Listing meeting your requirements and provide advice with your best interests in mind.

I know you're probably asking how buyer brokers get paid for the service they provide. They approach the listing real estate broker and say, "I have a potential buyer for your listed property. If the sale closes, will you share the commission with me?" The answer, of course, is "yes." The listing broker is in business to sell houses and shares commissions all the time.

Again, the big difference is that a traditional listing broker has a legal obligation to represent the seller's best interests while a buyer broker has a legal obligation to represent the buyer's best interests.

There is one more important consideration, in my opinion, when choosing any real estate agent.

Do they work full-time or part-time in the business?

Real estate professionals who get results are dedicated folks who spend long hours each and every day working for and with their customers or clients. They don't just sit around waiting for a phone call by someone who wants to see a property. Finding properties that fit a prospects needs requires a lot of work and typically a lot of showings.

Some people in the business don't have the time to devote because real estate is a second job for them or they have other obligations that cause this to be a part-time job.

In a nutshell, I think you are better served by a full-time real estate professional. And the same applies to home inspectors. By and large, professional, full time business people can better serve your needs than part-time hobbyists. And try to find someone who has been in the business for years, not months!

So who will you choose to work for you?

**BOTTOM LINE: Some real estate agents will try to convince you they can be double agents and will represent you as well as the seller. In view of the above discussion, does that make any sense to you?**

# Real Estate Agents and Home Inspectors — Like Oil and Water

Most Real estate agents are extroverted, friendly, happy and excited to be a part of the home buying process.

Home inspectors tend to be introspective, if not introverted. They are curious, serious, reflective and critical. And since they are paid to look for problems, their reports can appear to be negative.

Home inspections add another layer to the real estate process. Agents are busy with listings, marketing, showings, contracts, negotiations, financing, appraisals and closings. Many would rather not be further inconvenienced by dealing with a home inspection.

Traditional real estate agents are on the seller's side and home inspectors are on the buyer's side. It is easy to understand why conflicts arise, especially when one or the other forgets his or her role.

When problems are found, they must be dealt with. More work! Some agents react by fussing with the inspector. Shooting the messenger, as it were!

Real estate agents should not interfere with the inspection process (e.g. "This inspector doesn't know what he's talking about.") and home inspectors should not interfere in the selling process (e.g. "Don't buy this house!")

I can't even begin to count the number of times a real estate agent has challenged my findings or made negative or inappropriate comments during an inspection.

Here's an example:

Agent: "This is an old house and therefore it doesn't have to meet current code, right?"

Me: "It is grandfathered from the current code," I would explain, "because there was no such code when it was built. Nonetheless, this is a safety hazard and if someone is injured or killed because of it, you and I, along with everyone else in sight, will be sued if I fail to point it out — irrespective of any code or absence thereof."

And another example:

Agent: "If it is so dangerous, why hasn't anyone been hurt? After all, the house is 35 years old!"

Me: "Perhaps because, luckily, no one has yet put themselves in a dangerous position with respect to the hazard," I would respond. "A bare electrical wire, for example, won't hurt you unless you touch it. If you happen to be bare-footed on a damp basement floor when you do, chances are good you will be seriously hurt or even electrocuted."

And one more example:

Agent: "How can you say that receptacle is defective? I just plugged a lamp into it and it works fine."

Me: "In fact," I would explain, "a lamp will still light when the hot and neutral wires are reversed, but now the entire light socket is "hot" and this poses a potential safety hazard to someone handling the lamp."

Conditions adversely affecting safety or habitability *are* problems, pure and simple! Wishing them away is not helpful to anyone.

It's best for buyers to discard any statements made by real estate agents relative to the condition of a property. You are paying for a professional opinion from a home inspector who has no other duties and no axe to grind. Rely on that person to advise you on the condition of the property. Once identified, most problems can be fixed. Sweeping problems under the rug doesn't make them go away.

And it is best to just overlook the occasional real estate agent who "pooh-poohs" the home inspection industry or an inspector's findings. Most agents have no training or experience in construction or inspection, yet some foolishly allow themselves to get involved in the technical aspects of the inspection. And, they do so at their own jeopardy! Be careful who you listen to!

Sometimes when an inspector finds something wrong agents will call in "their handyman" to smooth over the findings or to perform a quick fix. Be sure you understand what the inspector found and that the person engaged to fix the problem is qualified to do so. Too many times I have seen slip-shod work or cosmetic repairs made by well-meaning but inept people. Most inspectors are happy to come back and re-inspect items after the repairs have been made for a modest fee. Again, don't rely solely on the agent to be sure the repairs are made correctly.

Please don't take this as a blanket indictment of all real estate folks. The realty industry is like every other profession, including home inspection. And, just like all other professional groups, such as doctors and lawyers, there are good practitioners, mediocre ones and disappointing ones.

Yes, some of my best and lifelong friends are real estate professionals and we have mutual respect for each other's roles in the real estate process. Know the proper role for each of the professionals you are working with and be aware of times when any of them stray over their appropriate boundaries.


**BOTTOM LINE: Agents and sellers should dialogue with inspectors to understand any reported deficiencies in a spirit of mutual cooperation aimed at resolving issues in the best interests of all parties. If conflict arises, things just tend to get worse.**

**Even though real estate agents may have powers of persuasion and may sound convincing, be aware that their job is not to understand or comment on the condition of a house. Your best bet is to rely only on the opinions of a professional home inspector regarding the condition of a property. If you are ever in doubt, get a second opinion from a qualified professional.**

# Tips on Selecting a Home Inspector

Many homebuyers place a great deal of trust in "their" real estate agents. So when the agent volunteers to take care of the inspection, many times the buyers agree. "I have an inspector I use all the time." may really mean "I have an inspector who never makes waves, never causes problems, never finds anything wrong — I really want you to use him!" But if there are any major problems, they need to be discovered. Nobody wants big surprises after they move in — or to wind up with a money pit! Before you accept an inspector recommended by a real estate agent, you should do some homework. Interview inspectors over the phone. Ask about their background and experience. "Are you a Certified ASHI Inspector?" "How many fee-paid inspections have you performed?" "Do you have errors and omissions insurance?" Then check them out with the Better Business Bureau. Find out how long they have been in business under their current name and how many unresolved complaints there have been.

One exception is when you're using a buyer broker. These brokers often recommend a home inspector they trust and with whom they have developed a good working relationship. One they can rely upon to meet their commitment to do what's in the best interest of their buyers. If a house has defects, they welcome disclosure. Things such as an unsafe electrical system, a furnace with a dangerous crack in its heat exchanger, or siding material which is known for poor performance and class-action law suits should not be overlooked. Once disclosed, the buyer broker has an obligation to get them resolved in a way that favors their client.

The second exception is when a traditional real estate agent says, "I know a home inspector who has a reputation for being thorough and objective and if there is something seriously wrong with this house he or she will find it." This is often the response when a buyer insists that they have a professional home inspection. They may have been "burned" before, or they may realize that there can be a big difference in the experience and competence of home inspectors. Or they may be professional engineers, architects, lawyers, doctors, corporate executives or even people in the home building industry who really do know that there can be a big difference among professionals. It is interesting to note that some of the real estate agents, who shuddered when I was engaged to inspect their listings, used me to inspect the homes and other properties they and their family members were buying.

The most important thing to remember is that all inspectors are not alike. The difference between them can be tremendous. For example, you can find someone who is new to the business, with little or no construction experience, who recently completed a one or two-week course on "How to Make Big Money as a Home Inspector." This person will likely compete on price, not quality. And you can expect to get what you pay for — very little for very little.

By contrast, you can find an inspector who has many years of experience in the home building industry, has performed thousands of fee-paid inspections, who acts in accordance with a recognized set of performance and ethical standards, who has errors and omissions insurance and a good record with the Better Business Bureau. Expect the professional to quote a higher fee; perhaps a lot higher. But, you can expect to get a lot more for your money. He or she will insist that you attend the inspection so that all of your questions can be answered. You will receive a well-written report, clearly defining any deficiencies along with remedial recommendations. In the long run, the professional will usually prove to be the bargain. One missed defect can cost you thousands to fix!

Which one will you pick? It's up to you. Do your homework. I always recommend Certified ASHI inspectors. Go to the American Society of Home Inspectors website (www.ashi.com) to locate members in your area. There can be differences even within this group of professionals so call them and ask the defining questions listed above.

**BOTTOM LINE: I've worked with attorneys on cases where inept home inspectors have missed big problems, and the buyer was suing the inspector. In one case in point, the inspector had no insurance, no money, and went bankrupt (oops!). The buyer wound up paying the lawyer <u>and</u> paying to fix the problem! Not a bargain!**

# "How Much Is a Home Inspection?"

When we received a call initiated with this question, an alarm went off. We knew the caller was not an educated home inspection consumer. Or, heaven forbid, they really were just looking for the cheapest inspection. In either case, it presented a challenge for us. Would we try to explain our service and emphasize that there can be a big difference in the quality of home inspections? Or, would we simply quote our fee, which would probably end the conversation?

Let me attempt to explain using a lesson I learned while renting apartments over the years. If someone called and asked, "How much is the rent?" We would respond that the unit was already rented. Why? Because it was clear to me that this type of person was not concerned about the apartment per se, just the price. Frankly, I saw these folks as people I'd rather not have as tenants.

Contrast that with someone who called to get information about an apartment. We would respond that they were newer construction, energy efficient, freshly painted with cleaned and sanitized carpets, etc. Then they would ask about cost, and if they had been doing comparative shopping, they would be very pleased with our competitive pricing for such a unit. Those were the kind of tenants I wanted. I offered them a quality unit at a justifiable price, not a cheap unit at a cheap price.

So it is in the home inspection business. People looking for a cheap inspection will get a cheap inspection. Some of my competitors did inspections for $99. Ours were quality inspections at a justifiable, but not by any means cheap price. A professional, well trained, well equipped, inspector with years of experience and insurance, cannot and will not compete on price. He or she will know what they are looking for, use a detailed yet easily understood reporting system and take the time to provide information and answer questions to help the client make an informed buying decision. It may cost more but it should also be worth much more. In my experience, the needed repairs I identified, which the client could ask the seller to cover, usually amounted to several times the cost of my inspection.

By any measure, my inspections were an excellent value even though they were usually more expensive than my competitors. After spending three or more hours in a house with my clients, they too were convinced that the information, service and personal attention provided was well worth my fee.

My business model was to receive a reasonable fee for the high quality product I delivered. That's what I did, and my business grew through referrals from satisfied clients. Having established a reputation for doing quality work, many of the buyers referred to us would not even ask about the fee, they just wanted to get on my calendar.

**BOTTOM LINE: The cost of dealing with a missed defect by a cheap, fly-by-night inspector can be much more than the cost of a professional inspection.**

# Home Inspector Licensing

Some states have enacted home inspector licensing laws. These vary in the amount and type of education, experience, testing, and insurance inspectors are required to have to obtain a license. What does this mean to you as a home buyer? First and foremost, understand that a license has little to do with the quality of an inspection. In fact, some of these laws tend to "dumb down" the profession, in my opinion, by establishing minimum requirements that are too easily satisfied.

Meeting the minimum requirements to become licensed means just that; it tells you that this person has the minimum knowledge and experience required to become licensed. No more and no less! It does NOT assure you of getting a professional home inspection. In fact, as I continue to emphasize, there can be a huge difference in the abilities of different home inspectors. In the final analysis, you are still the person who is going to have to decide which one can do the best job for you.

Licensing is good as far as it goes, because licensees are at least minimally qualified. But, look at other professional groups who are licensed. Doctors, lawyers, real estate agents, and even hair dressers are licensed. We have all heard horror stories about bad, albeit licensed, practitioners. Professional credentials, experience and reputation are far more important than a license hanging on the wall.

**BOTTOM LINE: If your state licenses home inspectors be sure you look beyond the license when selecting your home inspector.**

# ESPECIALLY FOR HOME INSPECTORS

## What Are Your Clients Paying For?

The short answer is knowledge. There is so much to know in the home inspection business that at times it almost becomes daunting. Home inspectors are called upon to inspect houses of all ages and must be familiar with decades, indeed centuries of evolving building practices and technology advances.

By contrast, a local code inspector must know only the specific code regulations currently in place in his area of administrative jurisdiction and must stay abreast of on-going code changes. Even that is not an easy task! But an independent home inspector must have the same working knowledge of codes and also must maintain a broad knowledge of building practices and building product failures over the years.

He or she must also be conversant in a number of other areas to identify problems where specialists may be required to enter the inspection process. It's not unlike a medical doctor, in general practice, who is trained in the broad medical profession and knows when a specialist may be needed. Some of the specialists that home inspectors routinely recommend are structural and geotechnical engineers, environmental specialists, landscape architects and entomologists.

Constant study and research is a way of life for practicing professionals like home inspectors. This is the knowledge base clients pay for when hiring a professional inspector. Knowledge is king in the home inspection business.

**BOTTOM LINE: Anyone can walk through a house and look at it, but it is the inspector's knowledge that makes this process meaningful. If a person does not know what to look at or does not understand what is observed, then he or she cannot make helpful, professional evaluations of the many elements of a property. If an inspector walks through a house with problems, he or she had better be able to identify them. And, if there are no problems, none had better be mistakenly called out! Like Yogi Berra once said, "It ain't what you know that will get you in trouble, but what you think you know that just ain't true!"**


## To Be or Not to Be

From time to time I'm called by an attorney asking me to testify in defense of a home inspector. Typically, the inspector is accused of failing to alert a client to a major defect.

Before committing to help in the inspector's defense, I ask the attorney for copies of all relevant documents pertaining to the claim. A review of this information helps me form an opinion as to whether there is a valid claim against the inspector. If the claim seems to be unsupportable, in my judgment, I will offer to participate.

On the other hand, I might be asked to testify against a home inspector. Again, I will review the case file to determine if the claim has merit. If so, I might participate.

By way of example, I was called upon to testify on behalf of an inspector who was accused of failing to disclose an alleged major foundation settlement problem. My review of the documentation, which included an evaluation by a structural engineer, very quickly revealed that indeed there was a serious problem that was not mentioned in the inspection report.

I explained to the attorney that the structural engineer's report described very large cracks and other visual evidence of severe foundation settlement. The attorney responded that "my client is not an engineer and his contract specifies that his inspections are only visual in nature." I responded by pointing out that the engineer's report contained no engineering analysis; it was merely a description of the visual evidence that he observed. Quite simply, two people looked at the foundation. One saw and reported large cracks; the other either didn't see the large cracks or failed to report them. I told him that I could not help him defend this inspector. In fact, I commented that I'd rather be on the other side of the case!

Inept or inexperienced inspectors put themselves in a very precarious position. They have a responsibility to their clients to observe, identify, explain and report defects. That is what the home inspection is all about. When major defects are overlooked or go unreported, inspectors can be sued. And they should not expect reputable, professional inspectors to come to their aid.

**BOTTOM LINE: The home inspection business is no place for inept, ill-prepared individuals. The risks are just too great!**

# What's A Professional?

Most home inspectors consider themselves professionals. In my opinion, a professional home inspector:

✓ Is first and foremost dedicated to providing the best possible service to his or her clients. Making money is an outcome, not a purpose!

✓ Conducts business in an ethically irreproachable manner.

✓ Stays current in all technical aspects of the business.

✓ Realizes that everything that's been learned is valuable and is willing, if not obligated, to pass this knowledge along for the sake of enhancing the profession. This is done by sharing information, mentoring, teaching, writing and publishing. True professionals leave something behind!

**BOTTOM LINE: Conducting one's business in a professional way not only benefits those with whom you interact, it provides a profound sense of personal satisfaction.**

# First Impressions

Professional inspectors will look professional. Arrive at the inspection site in a clean vehicle. Any lettering should be done professionally and should not be overdone — perhaps just the company name, phone number and a slogan. My market had a half dozen GM plants and so I chose to drive a GM truck; I wore out four of them. Be sensitive to your market when selecting a vehicle.

Personal appearance goes without saying — clean, neat and properly shaven. I always wore clean surgical booties inside houses.

Your demeanor can get things off to a good start. Introduce yourself with a hearty handshake and a smile. A little small talk about the weather or a positive comment about the neighborhood or your first impression of the house can help take the edge off for clients and sellers alike. If the seller has a dog, pet it. If kids are present, acknowledge them and comment on how cute they are. Give everyone a business card, even the kids – they really like being included!

**BOTTOM LINE: You don't get a second chance to make a first impression!**


# The Physical Side

When I first considered becoming a home inspector, my vision of what it entailed was a far cry from what I actually experienced once involved. After all, how difficult could it be? Walking through a house, making visual observations and producing a report will be a "piece of cake," I thought.

But, there is also a physical side to this business worth considering by anyone thinking about becoming a home inspector. Believe me, inspection work can be very physically demanding if it's done properly. Walking through a house is easy and usually safe. Crawling through attic and under-house crawl spaces is not. Walking on high-pitched roofs is especially uncomfortable and inherently dangerous. But these are requirements of the job!

I feel very fortunate to have survived twenty-five years of inspecting houses with only a few scars. I've fallen off of a roof, stepped on and been impaled on framing nails, been bitten by poisonous spiders and stung by angry wasps, had fingers stabbed by large splinters and crushed by faulty windows and doors. I've endured countless scalp punctures from exposed roofing nails. I've been trapped under a heating duct in a crawl space, trapped in an attic when the ladder collapsed and on a roof when the wind blew my ladder down. I've been covered with mud from head to toe, walked through 130° F attics and climbed trees and power poles to see inaccessible roofs when there was no other vantage point. I've been attacked and slobbered on by large dogs, bitten and clawed by cats, scared half to death by huge snakes, challenged by a mother raccoon and chased by farm animals. I've been cursed at by building contractors, real estate agents, lawyers and home owners. I've been exposed to asbestos, radon, mold, lead paint, toxic insulation, gas leaks, carbon monoxide and hideous odors.

Yes, the physical challenges in this business are numerous and challenging! It all comes with the job; "a piece of cake"!

**BOTTOM LINE: A professional makes it look easy! The home inspector's job is actually physically as well as mentally challenging if it's done right!**

# The Communication Side

Inspectors must practice good written and verbal communication skills as a vital part of the job. I used to tell my clients "If I leave this house knowing more about it than you do, I have not done my job." Here are the communication rules I developed and followed.

**RULE #1: Tell your client everything you discover!** Good things as well as bad things! This very simple rule must govern an inspector's communications with clients. What you observe in a house is not your information; it belongs to your client. And what you see must be described in a way that will be easily understood.

**RULE #2: Be sure you know what you are talking about before you talk about it!** There are four phases of reporting your inspection findings and they must be done in this order.

1. **Observe.** As you move through a property the bad stuff will jump out and grab you. If it doesn't, you're either not looking closely enough or you don't have enough experience to recognize bad stuff.
2. **Think.** Think about the anomaly you're viewing and how to best describe it to your client.
3. **Write.** Then enter it into your report as clearly and concisely as you can. Review what you've written and make any changes or improvements you feel necessary to adequately convey your finding.
4. **Speak.** Now you are ready to talk! You will not have blurted out the first thing that came into your mind! Instead, you will provide a well thought out, concise, and easily understandable description of the defect.

**RULE #3: Don't say or write anything that you wouldn't be able to defend in courtroom testimony.**

- **If you are providing factual information**, be able to back it up with credible reference material if and when the occasion ever arises.
- **If you're offering an opinion**, be sure to state that it is an opinion based upon your background and experience.

**RULE #4: Communicate in a way that is most appropriate for the particular client.**

I like to say that you wouldn't talk to your grandmother the same way you would talk to your 3 year old, or the same way you would talk to your wife, or the same way you would talk to your beer-drinking buddy. Assess your client's communication needs and respond accordingly.

Some clients want a lot of information. Their body language and questions will make their interest obvious. These people are probably extroverted and expressive. Give them all the information they want. Others, who might be introverted, are more reserved and thoughtful and may not outwardly signal their interest. These folks need time to process information, so present your findings and back away, giving them time to think things through.  Don't confuse their reticence with a lack of interest!  Periodically ask these clients if they have any questions throughout the process.  This allows them to think their questions through and know that you welcome their questions.


## RULE #5:  Stay focused and don't be distracted from looking at everything you need to look at.

A good checklist report can guide an inspector through all of the elements of a property.  I called mine a roadmap; it helped me ensure that I looked at, reported and discussed all of the important elements of a house.  Each item should also be evaluated.  I used columns to signify whether an element was "Functioning as Intended", "Minor Repairs Recommended", "Areas of Concern" or "Not Applicable/Not Inspected."  This is the essence of the report; it helps the client put the information into a context he or she can understand.  In addition to the rating, I used a "Comments" column to further define any relevant findings.  And, of course, I discussed my findings with the client as well.


## RULE #6:  Help your client understand what is wrong and how important it is.

To communicate effectively, inspectors must be able to explain and document areas of concern in easily understood, non-technical terms.  Explanations should be concise and to the point.  The component is "not functional,' or "not functioning as intended," or a "safety concern" or  "affects habitability."  This should be followed by a brief explanation of the condition.  For example: "The unit did not respond properly to user controls.", "It is a fire hazard.", "It is a potential shock hazard.", "The damp environment could support unhealthy mold growth." etc.  And remember, if it is your opinion based upon your background or experience; be sure to state it as such!


## RULE #7: Insist that your client attend their inspection.

Communication is such an essential part of the home inspection process that to the extent possible, I insisted that my clients attended their inspections.  As I explained things to them I could show them what I was talking about, read their body language as a gauge of their comprehension, use analogies to help them understand, ensure that they received the information, and put the information into proper context for them.

I could go on and on about the importance of communication.  In over two decades in the home inspection business I was never sued; not once!  I am convinced that good communication was a big part of that rarely achieved track record.


**BOTTOM LINE:  Remember that your product is <u>information</u> and <u>communication</u> is the delivery system.  A home inspector should never leave a house knowing more about it than his client. Communicate, communicate, and communicate!**

# THE Final BOTTOM LINE

## If you are buying a house:

✓ Do your homework. Have a good feel for what you want within the confines of your budget. Study neighborhoods and their schools, hospitals, churches, shopping, public services, crime rates, and health/recreation centers.

✓ Choose a real estate professional you trust. You don't have to call the one listed on the sign. Ask around. Consider using a buyer broker.

✓ Know the rules by which real estate professionals' play, so that you will be able to play the game to your best advantage.

✓ Get an inspection from a qualified home inspector; don't let anyone talk you out of it! You can find the ASHI Certified Inspectors in your area at www.ASHI.com.

## If you are selling a house:

✓ Deal with any problems disclosed with a rational approach.

✓ Consider getting a second opinion, in writing, from another professional.

✓ Fixing major problems is in your best interest, because even if you were unaware of their existence, you now have disclosure.

✓ If you choose to let this prospect walk for your failure to address the problem, you still face the issue of disclosure with subsequent prospects. Fraudulent non-disclosure can get nasty!

## If you own a house:

✓ Learn enough about how things work to be able to spot trouble before it gets out of hand.

✓ Maintain your house as though it could be put on the market for resale today. Deferred maintenance can be a big problem if and when you either want to, or have to sell.

✓ When things break, hire only repair contractors who have a reputation for good service, fairness and honesty, and always check repair people out with the Better Business Bureau.

# If you are a real estate agent:

✓ Accept that the home inspector's job is disclosure. It simply is what it is! Getting upset with the inspector won't make things better.

✓ Professional home inspectors can help you stay out of court.

✓ Refrain from offering your opinion on property conditions; that's not your job.

✓ Confrontations with home inspectors make things worse.

✓ Take the time to understand any deficiencies disclosed.

✓ When seeking a second opinion, be sure to get it in writing.

✓ Maintain a positive attitude; almost everything can be fixed.

# If you are a home inspector:

✓ Be the best you can be. You owe it to yourself!

✓ Hold yourself to the highest ethical standards. It will pay off!

✓ Work hard and don't take any short cuts. Shortcuts are the path to hell in the home inspection business!

✓ Financial gain is an outcome, not a goal. If you're good at what you do, monetary reward will follow!

✓ Compete on service and quality, not on price!

✓ Remember that communication is your **ONLY** product. Be good at it!

✓ Be fair to all parties in a transaction. Be totally objective and don't play games!

✓ Be ready to defend everything you put in a report. What you've heard, "old wives tales", and your personal hunches don't count! Just facts. (You can offer an opinion in a court of law only after the judge has accepted your credentials to testify as an expert on matters before the court, and even then you will be challenged!)

✓ Never stop learning! You can't possibly live long enough to know it all, but you can try!

✓ Share your professional knowledge. Mentor! Teach! Write! Publish!

✓ Be a leader and help raise the professional bar. Participate in ASHI!

✓ And, most of all — Be **INTREPID!**